SPONTANEOUS PLAY IN EARLY CHILDHOOD
from birth to six years

Spontaneous Play in Early Childhood

from birth to six years

Mary D. Sheridan

OBE, MA, MD, DCH, FFCM, LRAM (Speech)

Foreword by Professor Jack Tizard, PhD

NFER Publishing Company

Published by the NFER Publishing Company Ltd.,
Darville House, 2 Oxford Road East, Windsor,
Berks, SL4 1DF, England.

Registered Office: The Mere, Upton Park, Slough,
Berks.

First Published 1977
© Mary D. Sheridan 1977

ISBN 0 85633 122 8

Printed in Great Britain by
William Clowes & Sons Limited
London, Beccles and Colchester

Line illustrations by T. S. Graves
from the author's collection of original photographs

Cover design and layout by Ken Arlotte

Overseas distributors:
(USA)
Humanities Press Inc., 171 First Avenue,
Atlantic Highlands, New Jersey 07716, USA
(Canada)
Institute of Psychological Research Inc.,
34 Ouest, Rue Fleury Street West, Montreal,
Province of Quebec, H3L 1S9, Canada
(Australia)
ACER, Frederick Street, Hawthorn
Victoria, Australia 3122
(New Zealand)
NZCER, Education House, 178–182 Willis Street,
Wellington 1, New Zealand

Contents

SSH
R

Foreword 7

Foreword

by Professor Jack Tizard PhD

Dr Mary Sheridan has a special place in British paediatrics. She is our most senior *community* paediatrician, having been for 40 years a distinguished practitioner of the 'new type' of paediatrics the establishment of which, at local level, is one of the principal recommendations of the recently published Court Committee Report on the Child Health Services. Like nursery education and child care, community paediatrics is founded on 'knowledge of the nature and range of normal development'. And like its sister disciplines of education and child care it is concerned with the intellectual and social, as well as the physical and clinical needs of developing children, whether normal or handicapped.

In this deceptively simple book Dr Sheridan takes us through the main varieties of spontaneous play which children engage in during the first seven or so years of life. She spells out the functions of play, categorizes types of play, and distinguishes between play, work and drudgery, in ways that are illuminating and relevant both to students of child psychology and to practitioners whether they be parents, teachers, nurses or doctors. I know of no other book which gives a more vivid illustration of what is meant when we say that the essential feature of childhood is that it is the period of development.

Dr Sheridan bases her work on the behaviour of 'real children in real situations'. This has, of course, an immediate, intuitive appeal as a method of study – particularly when one is concerned with the engaging but restless, self-willed, non-verbal children of less than three years of age, or handicapped children of whatever age who share these same characteristics. In practice, however, research of this sort is extraordinarily difficult. It is not merely a matter of video cameras and tape recorders, though, as Dr Sheridan says, these are revolutionizing the study of behaviour in early childhood: much more important is an adequate theoretical framework, without which observation is mere entertainment. Dr Sheridan's observations are undistorted by theory; but her theoretical understanding of stages and processes of development enables her to interpret what she sees and records so clearly.

Both in her lectures and in this book Dr Sheridan uses pictures not merely to illustrate her argument, but to show visually what she also explains in words. Without the pictures the text would not achieve its purpose; without the text the pictures would have only a visual appeal.

Spontaneous Play in Early Childhood

can be read with profit and enjoyment by all students of child development. I hope it will become part of the recommended reading for all who are concerned with the upbringing and welfare of young children.

Reference
Child Health Services Committee (1976) *Fit for the Future* (Report of the Court Committee on Child Health Services). London: HMSO.

Jack Tizard
3rd January 1977

Section 1

DEFINITIONS RELATING TO PLAY

Introduction

In this book I have attempted to describe, illustrate and offer my personal interpretation of the main varieties of spontaneous play which engage the active interest of normal children from early infancy to about 7 years, with some of the more obvious implications for the understanding and encouragement of the play needs of handicapped children in corresponding phases of physical, mental and social development. It is intended to supplement the notes on play given in *Children's Developmental Progress* (Sheridan, 1975).

Unless specially differentiated, children of both sexes are referred to throughout as 'he'.

The book is divided into **Four Sections:**

Section 1 deals with definitions relating to play.

Section 2 deals with normal ages and stages in the development of play.

Section 3 provides outlines of some particularly significant play sequences.

Section 4 deals with play of handicapped children.

The illustrations have all been prepared by Tom S. Graves from my own large collection of colour slides. The original photographs were taken in completely unrehearsed and informal situations even when common test materials were employed.

Every child has the right to be cherished as an individual and encouraged to develop at his own pace, within the affection and security of his own family and the friendly acceptance of neighbours. Young, handicapped children have a special need for the constant, taken-for-granted, physical, mental, emotional and social stimulation that comes from being handled, talked to, applauded and played with and which is inherent in ordinary good child care. Since they are exceptionally demanding of attention, however, their parents, teachers and other care-givers require special guidance in their day-to-day management, in keeping them healthy and contented, and training them to move about safely, to occupy themselves profitably and to communicate effectively with their fellows.

Although, in common with all other young animals, children learn the basic rules of 'species behaviour', in other words the special life-style of human beings, from observation and imitation of their parents, human children alone are actively instructed by their elders. A child's integration into the social world is founded on two dominant inborn drives, to establish rewarding personal relationships with his fellow beings, and to learn essential everyday skills through various forms of play. In his play, a child experiments with people and things, stores his memory, studies causes and effects, reasons out problems, builds up a useful vocabulary, learns to control his self-centred emotional reactions and adapts his behaviours to the cultural habits of his social group. Play is as necessary to a child's full development of body, intellect and personality as are food, shelter, fresh air, exercise, rest and the prevention of illness and accidents to his continued mortal existence.

Provision of suitable *playthings*, *playspace*, *playtime* and *playfellows* for all young children and particularly for young handicapped children who cannot assist themselves, is therefore of primary importance.

To prevent any misunderstanding of my following discussions, I must make it clear from the onset that I write as a practical paediatrician and educationist, not as an experimental psychologist. All my professional inquiries during the past 40 years have been conducted at field level and directed towards producing some urgently needed clinical testing-procedure, which hopefully would also provide appropriate guide-lines for treatment. Empirical observational research of the sort I have been obliged to conduct is not founded in structured situations, controlled sampling, and computer analysis. Although I recognize the value of such studies for other purposes, long experience in hospitals, clinics, nurseries and every type of school, has taught me that the most detailed study of the work of learned theorists cannot provide understanding of real children in everyday situations, that there is no short-cut to clinical expertise, and that the only sure way to learn how to identify, assess and guide exceptional children in the earliest stage of deviance is to begin by acquiring factual knowledge of the nature and range of normal development. It was while studying the early development of vision, hearing and language that I came slowly to appreciate my need to consider the full paediatric and educational implications of the spontaneous play of very young normal children and, even more pertinently, the play of young, pre-verbal multi-handicapped children (Sheridan, 1975).

Medical literature was silent on the subject. Seeking help from other sources, I studied many old and new standard works on child psychology and education (Connolly and Bruner, 1972; Freud, 1955; Gesell, 1954; Head and Newson, 1976; Herron, 1971; Millar, 1968; Owen, 1975; Piaget, 1951; Richards, 1974; Schaffer, 1971; Tizard, 1976) and also on toy design (Lear, 1976; Matterson, 1965; Page, 1953), only to find that, while many careful, usually cross-sectional inquiries had been conducted concerning the play activity of numerically small groups of babies under 12 months (captive in cradles) and of children between 3 and 6 years (captive in nursery and infant schools), little fact-finding research of any sort had been carried out regarding the *spontaneous* play of children between 1 and 3 years. The reason for this apparent neglect was clear. Until the recent availability of small video-tape cameras (which are revolutionizing such studies) observations and recording of behaviour in unstructured situations of these engaging but restless, self-willed, non-verbal children raised formidable difficulties. The likelihood of obtaining observer agreement regarding the underlying meaning of their unpredictable activities and communications in relation to their psychomotor, cognitive, emotive and social development was even more improbable. But this developmental stage was precisely the one which I most needed to understand in order to prescribe remedial treatment and offer realistic guidance to the parents of young handicapped children. Moreover, I needed to know the normal developmental sequences in the play of babies and young children, and no such longterm follow-up studies were recorded. So I was obliged to go out and look for myself. Since I had little time to stop and stare, noting behavioural details usually had to be done in the course of my ordinary work. Only much later did I realize that what I now term 'fringe observation' was most valuable to my particular purpose since the behaviour of everyone concerned, myself included, was entirely natural. There is often considerable difference between the abilities a child registers under laboratory conditions and those spontaneously demonstrated in more homely circumstances. I soon found it advisable to discard high-sounding but ambiguous terms such as 'fantasy play', 'projective play' and 'symbolic substitution' in favour of plain words and straightforward description. In this way, I acquired hosts of vivid clinical impressions, which I noted down when I could and which experience slowly averaged and computed, providing broad generalizations regarding ages and stages. I also learned that any prediction with regard to the behaviour of human beings is uncertain, particularly of young, rapidly developing human beings in constantly changing situations, and that the best-intentioned observer's report can never be completely unbiassed.

Definitions

Basic definitions of play, work and drudgery were also lacking, but needing to distinguish between them for the purpose of my own deliberations and discussions I evolved the following:

Play is the eager engagement in pleasurable physical or mental effort to obtain emotional satisfaction.

Work is the voluntary engagement in disciplined physical or mental effort to obtain material benefit.

Drudgery is the enforced engagement in distasteful physical or mental effort to obtain the means of survival.

We all know that play and work may merge into each other (I would define this as *ploy*), and work and drudgery may also merge (would define this as *slog*), but play and drudgery are incompatible.

The everyday world of school children provides a foretaste of the adult world in that their daily work consists of uneven and fluctuating combinations of ploy, acquired competence and slog, just as our own work consists of varying amounts of exciting research, skilled practices, and pedestrian plodding; but all these variations confer a certain satisfaction since they are willingly undertaken and do not outrage human dignity.

These distinctions in the special educational treatment of handicapped children are important. Some of the so-called 'play', I have seen pressed upon handicapped children, always with the very best intentions, has been perilously near to drudgery.

Man's Unique Biological Achievements

Four outstanding biological achievements of homo sapiens mark his superiority over all other animals (Sheridan, 1975):

(a) upright posture, which facilitates locomotion and enables him to initiate, adapt and maintain an enormous variety of effective postures and movements while leaving his hands free for more precise activities;

(b) visual competence and uniquely flexible digits conferring ability to construct and use hand tools;

(c) possession of spoken language;

(d) evolution of complex cultural societies for the common benefit of the groups and individuals who comprise them, and for protection of the young of the species during their prolonged period of dependency.

A child's developmental progress may be conveniently observed and defined within the context of these biological parameters as follows:

Parallels of Human Development

Motor involving body postures and large movements. These combine high physical competence and economy of effort with precise forward planning in time and space.

Vision and Fine Movements involving competence in seeing and looking (far and near) and manipulative skills, integrating sensory, motor, tactile and proprioceptive activities.

Competence in *Hearing and Listening* and *the use of Codes of Communication*.

Social Behaviour and Spontaneous Play involving competence in organization of the self (i.e. self-identity, self-care and self-occupation), together with voluntary acceptance of cultural standards regarding personal behaviour and social demands.

Functions of Play

In childhood it is characteristic for the developing *body* to be continually but purposefully active, the developing *mind* to be alert and curious, and the developing *personality* to be eager to establish rewarding relationships with other people. Thus does a child become a healthy, useful, well-adjusted adult, knowing contentment and self-respect. *Play*, which provides suitable opportunities to strengthen the body, improve the mind, develop the personality and acquire social competence, is therefore as necessary for a child as food, warmth and protective care. It represents for him, according to his changing needs, moods and intentions:

Apprenticeship to independent living, i.e. continuity of practice leading to competence in everyday skills.

Research i.e. observation, exploration, speculation and discovery.

Occupational therapy, i.e. relief from pain, boredom or distress.

Recreation, i.e. simple, enjoyable fun.

Essential Provisions for Play

Four provisions are of primary importance – playthings, playspace, playtime and playmates.

Playthings must be appropriate for the child's age and stage of growth and development. They must be not too few or the child will lack stimulation, and not too many or he will become confused and unable to concentrate attention.

Playspace is needed for the 'free-ranging' activities, which are commonly shared with others, but every child must also possess a small personal 'territory' which he knows is his own and which therefore provides a secure home base. (Another type of 'personal space' which moves about with the child and is already clearly observable in the solo-play of ones-to-twos is discussed more fully in a later section.)

Playtime must be reasonably peaceful and predictable. It should be adequate for fulfilment of whatever activity is presently engaging the child's interest, without premature interruption likely to cause frustration, or undue prolongation leading to fading of purpose from boredom, loneliness or feeling of neglect.

Playfellows are required at all stages of development. Encouraging adults are not only essential to dependent infants but also in the period of *solo-play* which is characteristic of children under $2\frac{1}{2}$ years, who are still unaware of such abstract principles as equal rights, sharing and taking turns. Need for companionship proceeds, as social communications improve, through the small *family-type collectives* usually acceptable between $2\frac{1}{2}$ and 4 years to the wider *peer-group* play, characteristic of 4- to 6-year-olds, who are well able to hold their own in every sense of the word. In still later childhood, spontaneous peer-group play becomes progressively more elaborate and, a point of considerable significance, more strictly disciplined according to agreed regulations, observance of which provides most of the enjoyable element. Between 7 and 12 years, leisure-time activities become more selectively sex-determined. Outdoor games, particularly role playing activities tend to be played in exclusive masculine gangs and feminine pairs or small groups. Male and female adolescents rediscover mutual common interests and gravitate into mixed groups again.

The leisure-time occupations of adults include all sorts of sports, hobbies, arts, crafts, even further education and good works. It is noteworthy that individual tastes and particularly artistic 'gifts' become obvious very early in life. They are often clearly apparent by seven or eight years of age.

Types of Play

Play begins spontaneously as soon as a child is released from the impositions of his primary neonatal reflexes. There is general agreement that its satisfactory development depends upon continuing adult encouragement and the provision of suitable toys and other equipment. There is less harmony of opinion regarding categorization.

My own purposes are best served by adherence to the old classification of six main types in relation to play of young children, but I would add a seventh category relating to older children and adults. The first types may be designated as follows: active, exploratory, imitative, constructive (or end-producing), make-believe and games-with-rules (win/lose) play. My seventh category is given the general title of hobbies. It includes all the various leisure-time pursuits which engage the interest of older persons of all ages.

These different types of play emerge in orderly developmental sequence as the child learns to use first his sensory and motor equipment to best advantage and later his powers of communication and creativity. Every step forward depends upon successful achievement of previous stepping-stones. They are discussed in detail later.

Some authorities distinguish 2 main types according to *function*, each with numerous sub-groups; 'mastery play' or 'work-play' which would include my 'apprenticeship' and 'research' categories, and 'ludic' or 'play-play' which would include my 'therapeutic' and 'fun' groups. It is considered that the distinction between work-play and play-play is usually clear to the child himself.

Other authorities prefer to classify the varieties of play according to a child's capacities for *socialization* with age-peers, as follows: diffuse (infantile), solitary, parallel, onlooker and co-operative.

Viewed from these premises, my own seven-fold classification might also be resolved into two main groups, although under the somewhat different headings of 'play of competence' and 'play of communication'. (It might equally be resolved into 'play for skills' and 'play for socialization'.)

In order of appearance and quality of performance, a child's playtime accomplishments closely reflect his normal developmental progress. Every step forward depends upon achievement and consolidation of previous gains in the same developmental parameter. Although their beginnings are readily distinguishable the main types of play soon become inseparably integrated. They fall naturally into two groups, those mainly concerned with bodily skills and those mainly concerned with human communications.

1 **Active play** presumes 'gross motor' control of head, trunk and limbs in sitting, crawling, standing, running, climbing, jumping, throwing, kicking, catching and so on. It is directly concerned with promotion of physical development and necessitates the provision of adequate free-ranging space to move about in, and natural obstacles to overcome, together with simple, safe, playground equipment, mobile and fixed.

2 **Exploratory and manipulative play** beginning at about 3 months with finger play, presumes possession of age-appropriate integration of gross-motor, fine-motor and sensory functioning. These components are essential not only for acquisition of hand-eye co-ordination, but also for attending to and localizing everyday sounds, for recognition of the permanence of objects and for learning to appreciate the implications of space and time. Integration of

these separate physical and cognitive elements into total meaningful experience necessitates the availability of a number of simple things for manipulation, such as everyday domestic objects, feeding and toilet articles, as well as traditional playthings like rattles, dolls, balls, building blocks, boxes, toys to grasp and move about by hand, and sound-making instruments.

3   **Imitative play** beginning very early in momentary episodes, becomes clearly evident from 7–9 months. It presumes a child's ability to control his body, manipulate objects, integrate and interpret multi-sensorial experience and comprehend simple language, or perhaps, more accurately, his caregivers' vocal tunes. It reflects what a child sees and hears going on around him, particularly in everyday social situations, providing a lively record of his perceptual learning (Schaffer, 1971). At first, this imitation is fragmentary and follows immediately upon the child's attention being attracted in some way to the activity which he imitates – usually a functional activity, personally experienced many times. Later he recalls and repeats for his own amusement or for applause a whole series of these meaningful actions and at increasingly longer

intervals. Imitative play is necessary in order for a child not only to learn the quickest and most effective way of performing meaningful actions himself, but also gradually to understand that adults have differing roles and responsibilities, because he has come to know first *how* and later *why* they carry out the activities he imitates. Hence it necessitates continual opportunity to observe living 'models' using a variety of common domestic objects, which will encourage his own explorations and manipulations. At the toddler stage he may be further stimulated to imitate by being given and shown how to use a few simple 'educational' toys for pushing, pulling, hammering, fitting pegs into holes, shaped blocks into their appointed places, etc.

4   **Constructive (or end-product) play** beginning with very simple block-building at about 18–20 months, presumes possession of all the fore-mentioned motor and sensory abilities together with increasing capacity to make use of the intellectual processes involved in recognition and retrieval of previously stored memories. Additionally, it requires ability to create preliminary 'blue-prints' in the mind and realize these in practical form. This type

of play grows directly out of early exploratory and manipulative play, but also implies capacity to combine early 'pure' imitation with primitive insight and purposeful anticipation. It is at this stage that the range of 'educational' toys and equipment provided in playgroups and nursery schools is of greatest value.

5   **Make-believe (or pretend) play** beginning a couple of months before 2 years and elaborated for several years afterwards, presumes previous acquisition of all the foregoing types, particularly imitative role play. Having learned from experience the probable causes and effects relating to the activities he has observed and copied, a child now deliberately invents increasingly complex make-believe situations for himself, in order to practise and enjoy his acquired insights and skills. In this way he offers his comments upon the passing scene, improves his general knowledge and, most importantly of all, refines his social communications. Make-believe play necessitates the availability of every sort of manoeuvrable material, including a judicious selection of durable, commercially-produced toys. Make-believe play depends upon a child's ability to receive and express his ideas in some form of language-code. Consequently its

spontaneous employment is of considerable diagnostic significance to professional workers concerned with the health, welfare and education of young children. This matter receives further discussion later.

6 **Games-with-rules** presuppose a high degree of skill in all the foregoing types including full understanding and acceptance of the abstractions involved in sharing, taking turns, fair play and accurate recording of results. They usually start at about four years when small groups of peer-age children, under tacitly acknowledged leadership, improvise their own rules for co-operative play. Team games, which challenge competitiveness in older children and adults, become increasingly subject to rules imposed from without and, to be rewarding, must be played strictly according to the recognized constitution.

Sophisticated recreations are beyond the scope of my present thesis. They include *hobbies* of every sort which continue to give pleasure throughout life.

Safety Measures

There is no need to stress the importance of ensuring that playthings for young children must be safe to suck, handle and drop, impossible to swallow, washable and as unbreakable as possible. Playspace must be homely, warm and free from hazard. The use of outdoor playground equipment is to be encouraged, provided suitable supervision is available.

Acknowledgements

It would be impossible adequately to thank all the friends and colleagues who have helped me, over many years, to obtain the photographs from which Tom S. Graves has prepared the illustrations to this book. My gratitude goes to them, and also to the parents who so freely gave their consent, but most of all to the children. They generously welcomed me into their play-world, then paid me the supreme compliment of completely ignoring my existence.

Mary D Sheridan

Section 2

NORMAL AGES AND STAGES IN THE DEVELOPMENT OF PLAY

In order to interpret the play of young children, particularly of exceptional children, and make suitable provision for their needs, it is appropriate to consider the ages and stages of development at which various significant manifestations of behaviour usually appear. It is important to bear in mind that wide individual differences are to be expected, and that for the sake of brevity, numerous intermediate phases and transitions are necessarily omitted here. Actual ages at time of photography are recorded underneath the illustrations. They are not necessarily the earliest age at which the indicated play appears.

3–6 months

The newborn baby does not need to be taught to move his limbs, to suck or to cry and he quickly learns to attract and welcome his caregivers' attentions. His mother is usually his first playmate. Although the young infant's vigorous movements, smiles, and coos when handled and talked to, obviously indicate responses to enjoyable stimulation, what is commonly regarded as 'true' play, in the form of purposefully-directed, visually-controlled reaching for toys, becomes possible only with the disappearance of certain primitive

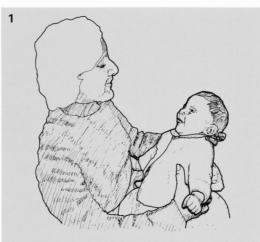

6 weeks A baby's first playmate is his mother. This lively interchange involves simultaneous looking, listening, vocalizing and bodily movement.

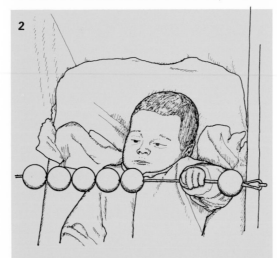

10 weeks She can grasp the bar and at the same time converge her eyes on a coloured ball, but is not yet able to co-ordinate hand and eyes.

reflexes unnecessary to describe here. Henceforth play is no longer merely a manifestation of stimulus and predictable response but increasingly a question of selective sensory intake (reception) which is then processed within the brain (interpretation) and results in some appropriate motor outcome (expression). Hand-eye co-ordination is demonstrated at about 10–12 weeks of age when a recumbent child, head in mid-line, deliberately brings his hands together over his upper chest and, converging his eyes upon them, engages in active interlacing finger-play. About the same time, when lying on his stomach holding his head and shoulders up steadily, he will open and shut his hands, scratching at the surface on which he lies, obviously with some appreciation of the simultaneous production of sight and sound. Given a holdable toy (such as a rattle or wooden spoon) he clasps it firmly and brings it towards his face, sometimes bashing his chin, but usually any glances he makes at it are fleeting. He finds it difficult to control his head, neck and eye muscles, and keep his hand in 'static' grasp at one and the same time. By about 14 weeks, however, he can hold the toy and steadily regard it. At about 18–20 weeks he can reach for and grasp an offered rattle, look at it with prolonged gaze and shake it. He can also take it to his mouth and then withdraw it. He can hold it between his two hands, clasping and unclasping it alternately. He can drop it by opening both hands wide, but cannot yet place it down neatly and deliberately.

By **6 months** his general neuro-muscular control, manipulation, stereo-scopic vision and hand-eye co-ordination are so advanced that he can reach out for and seize hold of any play object within reach of his extended arms. He has discovered the possession of feet and often uses them as auxiliary claspers. He brings every grasped object to his mouth. He is still incapable of voluntary hand release. He recognizes meaningful objects when they recur in situational context. He is beginning to comprehend the permanence of *people* but not yet the permanence of *things*. When a toy falls from his hand, unless it is within his continuing range of vision, it ceases to exist for him.

3 **12 weeks** Lying on his front, lifting his head and resting on his forearms he scratches at the table cover enjoying the simultaneous sight and sound of his finger movements.

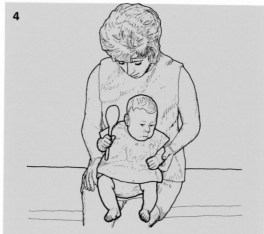

4 **12 weeks** Held sitting he grasps the wooden spoon handle firmly but is still unable to give his plaything simultaneous visual attention.

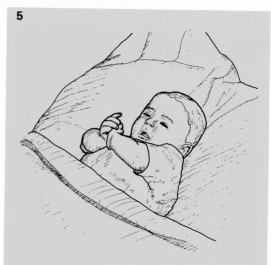

5 **3 months** With head and back well supported she demonstrates good hand/eye co-ordination in finger play.

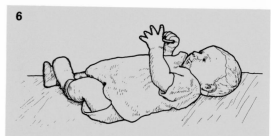

6 **4½ months** With the attainment of consistent hand/eye co-ordination he holds the teething ring between his hands, opening and closing them alternately.

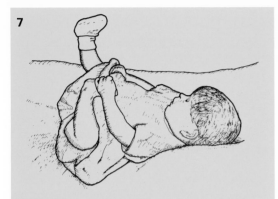

5½ months Having discovered his possession of feet, he brings his extended legs into vertical position and reaches out in foot/eye co-ordination.

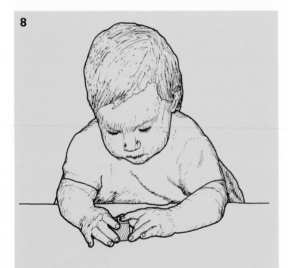

6 months With an expression denoting high concentration, he makes characteristic age-related two-handed approach to a block. (Immediately after this he took it to his mouth.)

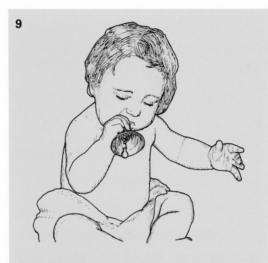

6 months Having grasped the base of the upturned bell with both hands and transferred it to her right hand she brings the prominent handle to her mouth.

6–12 months

At about **7 months** he begins to appreciate the functional 'twoness' of hands and a week or two later, of feet. He can hold two objects, one in each hand simultaneously using firm palmar grasp and bring his hands together to 'match' them. He can now pass a toy from one hand to the other with voluntary hand release. From about 8 months he sits steadily on the floor, stretches out in all directions for toys within his arm's reach without falling over, and begins to creep and reach towards eye-catching objects. He clearly demonstrates ability to differentiate between familiar people and unfamiliar strangers at about 7 months. About 9–10 months he becomes aware of the permanence of objects because he will lift a cushion to look underneath it for a plaything which, while he watches, first has been half-hidden, i.e. with a part of it showing and, two or three weeks later, wholly covered. He leans over the side of his pram to keep a falling plaything in view. He begins to throw toys about for the satisfaction not only of motor achievement, but for the interest of seeing and hearing the sequence of events which occur when objects fall, roll away and come to a standstill. He enjoys producing the simultaneous noise and tactile sensation of banging or sliding about solid objects such as blocks, bells or small domestic items, on hard flat surfaces.

At about **9 months** he usually first regards a new toy appraisingly for a few moments, as if to judge its qualities, before reaching for it. He prefers to concentrate on one toy at a time, manipulating it carefully. A little later, from imitation or discovery, he can combine 2 objects in some active way, such as banging a couple of wooden spoons together – clicking blocks, or rattling a spoon in a cup. It is noteworthy that in this respect girls tend to be a little more advanced than boys, but boys may already show more vigorous locomotor activity. At this stage, in both boys and girls, preliminary regard of playthings before eager seizure is briefer and mouthing of toys is lessening. At 12 months, girls also tend to engage in 'give and take' play with caregivers, but boys usually not until somewhat later, although boys often show more interest than girls in simple ball games, rolling and throwing from a sitting position.

All babies, as they become more mobile, increasingly seek proximity to their mother, partly for the reassurance of her constant availability and partly to seek her co-operation in play. By now

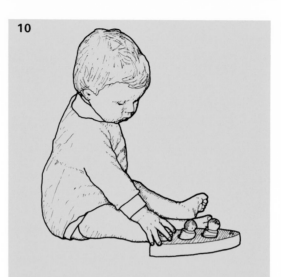

9 months   Sitting competently on the floor he reaches sideways to take the pegmen from their holes. He is not yet able to replace them.

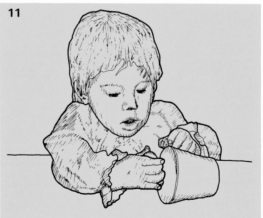

9 months   Although she is not yet able to release the blocks into the cup she has some notion of the nature of container and contained and keeps on trying.

9 months   Having watched her playmate build a tower of blocks for her to knock over, she tries to imitate. Grasping right hand and pointing left index finger are well shown.

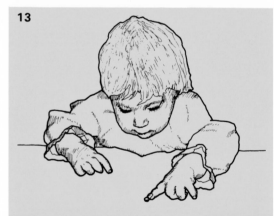

9 months   This poking at a small sugar pellet with one index finger is characteristic for this age, so too is the 'mirror' posture of the other hand.

14

10 months Creeping towards an eye-catching plaything and reaching for it (note persistence of the same posture in Fig. 83).

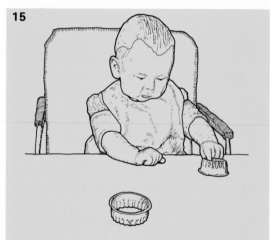

15

10 months Enjoying the simultaneous sight and sound made by sliding plastic pastry cutters on his wooden table.

16

11 months Having acquired the ability to crawl, he is exploring and exploiting the exciting possibilities of the domestic environment.

17

11 months He improves his skill in loco-motion by carrying two objects simultaneously. *Note:* Babies do not distinguish between porcelain and plastic.

she is so necessary to them that they are distressed if she leaves the room outside the range of sight and hearing.

From **9–12 months**, he has clearly begun to understand the import of his mother's spoken communications: first the cadences of her vocal intonation, then of a few single word-forms and eventually of the simply phrased in-structions and prohibitions which are addressed to him personally in recurrent situational context. He is beginning to find meaning in his homely world. He likes to watch and listen to his familiar adults as they go about their daily occu-pations and periodically to be touched, talked to and played with as they pass. Like every other young animal, his early learning depends upon the quantity and quality of this affectionate, taken-for-granted, one-to-one mother-teaching at mother-distance. His attentions, re-lationships and play are still engaged and satisfied mainly at the level of on-going perceptions, but his immediate, brief imitations indicate that he has come into possession of a short-term memory and is proceeding with the establishment of a long-term memory-bank. For the latter, he will gradually pile up all sorts of memoranda related to significant somatic, cognitive and affective experiences, for the purpose of instantaneous recognition, retrieval and creative assembly when he needs them.

Because of its reliance on percepts rather than concepts, early play may remain endlessly repetitive unless the mother indicates the next step. This she usually does instinctively, but not always. A non-participating mother therefore needs help to understand her own essential part in the furtherance of her child's optimal development. Professional workers also need reminding that a mother in the ordinary home cannot just stop what she is doing in order to play with her child, but her encouragement towards his independent mobility and her frequent affectionate communications, however brief, are all-important in promoting his competence. In these homely ways, a child learns during his first year that *things* keep their properties even in movement, but the behaviour of *people* tends to be most interestingly, though not frighteningly, unpredictable. He must be able to move about his familiar world so as to acquire a working knowledge of its nature and its possibilities. He must also learn to acquire a measure of control over his own behaviours and relationships within it, before he can communicate his wishes, attitudes and intentions with regard to it.

At home, a child balances his need for close proximity to his mother with his need to explore, nicely integrating motor activity with sensory alertness and emotional satisfaction. He also recognizes situational constancy in home surroundings. For instance, he knows that if his mother is busy at the kitchen sink she will not suddenly disappear beyond his power to summon her back, as she might do say in the open park. He can therefore begin to tolerate extending intervals of time and space between them.

(*Note:* Appropriate playthings for these first stages of development have already been briefly discussed in the previous section. They are also illustrated in the pictures accompanying this section.)

In his first 12 months a baby has already travelled a far distance from early dominance by neonatal reflexes, to his present individualistic manifestations of capability and personality. If he is to achieve his full potential he must be helped to travel even further and more rapidly during the next couple of years.

11 months His first steps require parental encouragement in word and deed and considerable courage on his own part.

11 months Confident in the secure grasp of her father's strong hand, she leans outwards to regard the view from the window.

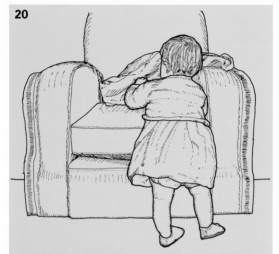

12 months Holding on to the furniture and stepping sideways she cruises about the room, investigating every object of interest en route — particularly parcels and receptacles.

12 months Boy. The kitchen provides many exciting — sometimes dangerous — possibilities for gathering everyday experiences. His watchful mother is close at hand, and fortunately the front door bell did not summon her away.

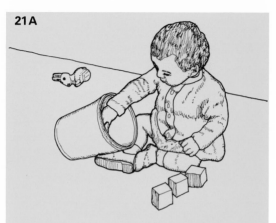

14 months Boy. Having gained some appreciation of the phenomenon of container and contained, he greatly enjoys putting objects in and out of the wastepaper bin.

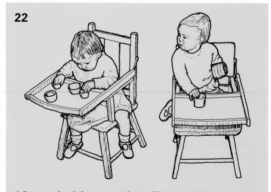

12 and 14 months These babies in a residential nursery awaiting their midday meal are sensibly improving the opportunity for manipulative and imitative play.

12–18 months

In this period a child becomes increasingly mobile, inquisitive, self-willed and difficult to control. His world of attention is rapidly expanding. He is no longer satisfied with his former lively acceptance of mainly perceptual phenomena but quickly loses interest in events which are presented to him mainly as distant, repetitious, unrewarding, visual displays and sound sequences. He needs to take a closer look at and a more active part in what is happening. This is shown by his obvious dawning recognition of cause and effect. This understanding is first manifest in his prompt imitation of activities repeatedly experienced in his own person, i.e. a sort of 'action-echolalia'. From this stage he proceeds to demonstrate more obvious and prolonged 'definition-by-use' in relation to common objects, such as drinking from an empty cup bringing a brush to his hair, etc. At first, these activities are very brief, but soon they become more extended in scope and in time, sequentially correct and directed towards some purposeful activity, i.e. an 'aim-in-view'. He is dominated by an urge to explore and exploit his environment. He is rapidly discovering the implications of container and contained. He looks into boxes and cupboards, to manipulate, smell and taste the objects within, sometimes presenting them to his mother, occasionally making some show of replacing them, but more often scattering them round the floor. He manipulates blocks with good pincer grasp but seldom aligns more than two or three together on the flat or in a 'tower', in imitation or spontaneously.

He still employs percussion tools to experiment in the synchronization of sound and strike. He tears papers to enjoy the simultaneous feel, sound and sight of this activity. As the weeks go by, with increasing skill in upright ambulation and navigation, he pushes and pulls large wheeled toys and guides small ones by hand or on the end of a string. He uses his trucks to transport collections of objects from one place to another, deliberately increasing the weight and complexity of his loads and the size of his stockpiles.

He still throws his toys about, but less often, and mainly as an expression of annoyance or to discard them when they cease to interest him, usually evidencing a large unconcern for direction or place of fall. His interests are still closely tied to everyday family and domestic realities. He begins to engage in short episodes of role play. He greatly enjoys active use of

23

12 months She holds the pencil in an age-typical fashion. A few moments later she shifted the pencil to the other hand.

24

12 months Having thrown out all his playthings he calls loudly for their restitution. This behaviour is not mere naughtiness but active time and motion discovery.

25

12 months This give and take play involved not only playthings but linguistic interchange.

26

12 months and 2 years These two little cousins meet every day and frequently engage in similar brief co-operative play while their mothers chat.

27

12 months She cannot yet name these objects but she is well able to demonstrate their use in relation to herself.

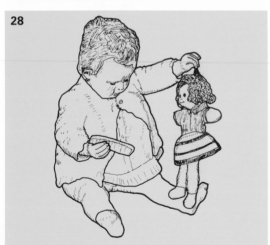

28

12 months She also has a vague notion of their application outside herself but cannot quite resolve the problem.

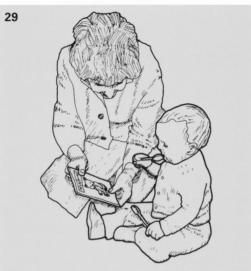

29

12 months Boy. This interest in books showing up very early is greatly encouraged by his mother. Meanwhile his two wooden spoons were not completely deprived of attention.

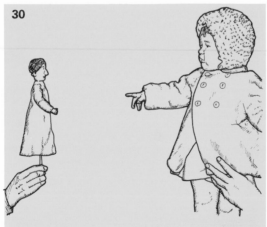

30

13 months Girl. The puppet evokes delighted pointing and loud vocalization and she is obviously anxious to share her excitement.

ordinary or 'Wendy-house'-sized replicas of familiar household objects like shopping baskets, sweeping brushes, pails, cups and saucers, pots, pans, telephones, furniture and garden tools. He manages to communicate his needs and feelings quite effectively in a medley of large expressive gestures, loud, tuneful vocalizations and a small, but ever-increasing repertoire of single words. He shows growing interest in naming objects and pictures, in repeating words and in listening to people talking (Sheridan, 1976).

At this developmental stage of limited cognitive, social and language appreciation *a doll or animal toy is treated like any other plaything*. Although he likes to carry one about with him everywhere, may name (i.e. verbally label) it correctly and strongly resist being dispossessed of it because it is his personal belonging, as yet it holds no true *emotional* significance as a symbol of a loved, animate being. Owing to immature preoccupation with the 'me' and only very primitive realization of the 'not me', he tends to treat live animals and other children, including his infant siblings, with similar apparent lack of affection or protective concern. A young child quickly learns that living creatures usually *do* things to him with some intention, while objects do not.

Consequently, so far as he is concerned, young babies, who do not 'intend' anything towards him, are, not yet living personalities in their own right, but merely objects to be manipulated, pushed about or rejected as the whim takes him. Behaviour that sometimes appears to the adult onlooker to be due to 'sibling jealousy' is much more likely due to lack of the concept of inter-familial relationships, unrealized because at this age inexplicable and incomprehensible. Social learning is undoubtedly entirely ego-centrated at first, i.e. 'self-tied', rather than 'self-ish'. This would explain why his early 'definition-by-use' directly shadows constantly applied activities of his everyday care, e.g. the use of feeding utensils, toilet articles and items of clothing. Acceptable externalized or 'detached-from-self' activities, leading later to the practice of unselfishness, sharing, taking turns and eventually to compassionate behaviour does not, indeed cannot, develop until a child has learned first the primary distinction of 'me' and 'not me', then the distinction of 'me' and 'you', and finally the distinction of 'us' and 'them', which is the keystone of social communication. Some at least of this learning depends upon appreciation of what is 'mine' and what is 'not mine', and of what is 'yours'

31

15 months Boy. By this time he clearly understands the functions of a comb and speaks a recognizable version of the word.

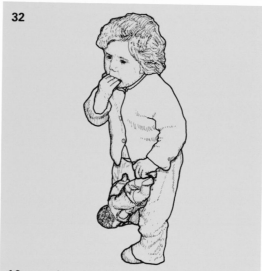

32

16 months Girl. She does not realize that dolls represent real babies to be loved and cared for. This is not cruelty or sibling jealousy, but immaturity.

33

15 months Boy. Already demonstrating the usual male pre-occupation with objects of transport, but solving problems of linkage are still beyond his capacity.

34

15 months Squatting on the floor he studies the picture book with interest, but turning several pages at a time.

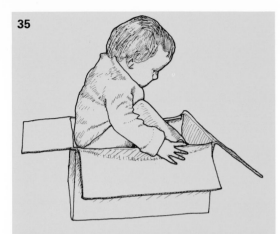

20 months Boy. Like all children of this age, he has an irresistible urge to get in and out of large boxes, perhaps learning his own relative size and position.

20 months He obviously enjoys the simultaneous sight and sound and muscular precision of his hammering activity.

and 'theirs'.

Until this final stage of cognitive and emotive maturation has been reached the child's egocentricity leads him to the unshakeable conviction that, as a matter of course, all things rightfully belong to him. His philosophy might be stated as being 'I come, I see, I grab' and 'What I have, I hold'. The lesson for caregivers is obvious. As soon as he is mobile he should be provided with some playthings and a place (for territory) which are indisputably his own, so that he may learn not only the satisfactions but the accepted conventions of personal and territorial possession including the need to respect the rights of others.

18–24 months

Between 18 and 24 months with rapidly improving control of his body and limbs a child engages in many gross-motor activities such as pushing, pulling and carrying of large objects, climbing on furniture, low walls and steps. Sitting on a small tricycle he can steer it on course, but propels it forwards with feet on the ground. His explorations are endless and since his sense of danger, like his understanding and use of language, are still very limited, while his desire for independent action is boundless, he requires constant supervision to protect him from danger.

He becomes increasingly interested in the nature and detailed exploitation of small objects, girls usually manifesting this curiosity somewhat earlier than boys. He opens handbags, boxes and drawers, rummaging among the contents, throwing some objects away, pulling others to pieces, tearing off wrappers, banging, hammering, poking, and generally practising his rapidly refining manipulative abilities. Given three or four suitable, durable toys like building blocks, model cars, wooden trains which link together, pegmen which fit into holes in moveable boats or roundabouts, sturdy dolls and teddy bears and a selection of simple 'educational' toys, he will play contentedly at floor level for prolonged periods, provided he knows that a familiar and attentive adult is near. He likes putting small toys in and out of containers. Once he has discovered or been given the idea, he builds towers of blocks varying from 3 at 18 months to 6 or more at 2 years. He experiments for lengthening periods of time with elemental substances like water and sand, or mouldable materials like clay and dough, using his hands and simple tools effectively, but as yet, without ability to plan or achieve an end-product.

His drawings are still in the nature of widespread brushwork demanding good co-ordination of hand and eye but lacking pictorial representation. His manipulations of pencils and paint-brushes show increasingly competent use of the fingers and thumb in the dynamic tripod (Rosenbloom and Horton, 1971) and although one hand is tending to show dominance, such preference is still very variable and he continues to use either hand freely and sometimes both together. These manifestations of unequal, shifting or perhaps non-simultaneous appreciation and control of laterality, continue with decreasing frequency throughout the pre-school years. The reason for this uncertainty remains unclear. It may have something to do with a need to build up one's 'body image' separately in the two sides of the brain.

He shows by his correctly serialized imitations of familiar adult activities that he already possesses a useful stock of sensory and kinesic memoranda, although these still remain centred on himself as the hub of his universe.

In the early role and situational 'pretend' play which is characteristic of this stage, he uses materials ready to hand, but in a fragmentary way. For instance, while playing for a few moments pretending to put himself to bed, he lies

37

18 months   Boy. The marvellous discovery of control of a push-and-pull toy could not be more clearly demonstrated.

38

18 months   A few weeks older; this boy can walk backwards and sideways, pulling and steering a trolley containing a collection of bricks.

39

19 months   He crawls swiftly up the garden steps. (The usual sequence of movements — R. hand, L. foot; L. hand, R. foot, is clearly shown.)

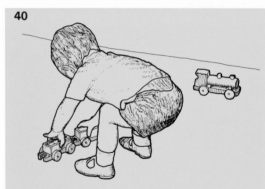

40

18 months   This boy, 3 months older than the boy in Fig. 33, playing with the same toys, is able to solve the linkage problem.

down, closes his eyes and pulls a cover over himself, but only if cushions or coverings are available. He goes through the movements of driving a car usually making suitable engine noises, if he has a seat and a steering wheel of sorts. He pretends to read a book if one is there. He puts two or three toys together

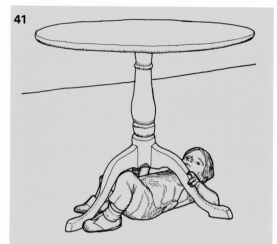

2 years Having competently assumed this position, he delightedly calls attention to the facts and implications of the situation.

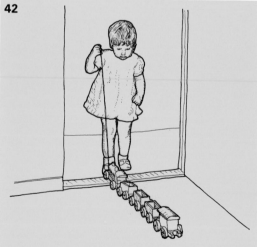

2 years Having successfully linked up the trucks, she pulls the whole train through the doorway, walking backwards and round the corner.

2½ years Having tried unsuccessfully to step into the train herself, she is still a little confused regarding the relative size of truck and teddy.

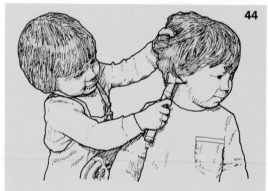

2 years Role play beautifully demonstrated by the doctor's son.

meaningfully, a doll on a chair, or bricks in a truck, but seldom, as yet, making one object represent another or using mime to symbolize absent things or events.

By 18 months he usually speaks a few single words such as 'tup' (cup), 'dink' (drink), 'baw' (ball), 'loo' (look), 'der' (there), 'uh' (up), 'dow' (down), in appropriate context and a number of meaningful utterances (holophrases) which to him are single words, such as 'gimme' (give me), 'hee-ya' (here you are), 'awgone' (all gone), 'der-ti' (there it is) 'do-way' (go away) or, in questioning cadence, 'wha-da' (what's that?). His intonations greatly help intelligibility, but in order to be sure of what he is saying it is necessary to know what he is actually doing. About 21 months he begins to put 2 or more 'real' words together to frame little sentences. These usually refer to very familiar matters, or to needs and happenings in the 'here and now'. He effectively communicates his wishes, refusals, likes and dislikes using a combination of finger-pointings, hand-pullings and urgent vocalizations, with a few words and phrases thrown in. He comprehends most of the simple language addressed to him but his store of evokable language symbols, which I prefer to call 'codemes' (Sheridan, 1972) is as yet very meagre.

Girls begin to treat their dolls in caregiving fashion at about 18–20 months, boys a little later. At about 21 months both begin to demonstrate their appreciation that *miniature toys* (i.e. dolls'-house-size) represent things and people in the real world. They clearly show this externalization (or expression) of previously internalized (i.e. memorized) experiences, by spontaneously arranging the little toys in meaningful groups, by actively indicating their use in everyday situations, and often by simultaneously talking about them. It is noteworthy that from the outset girls show preference for play with domestic objects, and boys for miniature cars and other items of transport. This type of play, which extends rapidly after 2 years, has proved of considerable help to me in the differential diagnosis of delays in the development of spoken language (Sheridan, 1968; 1972; 1976).

Lowe's recently published findings in relation to her own miniature toys test (Lowe 1975) are in complete accordance with my own observations.

For some time however, although they correctly name and delicately manipulate these tiny toys, both boys and girls remain somewhat confused regarding the size of the toys in relation to themselves, so that they will try to sit on a miniature chair, to ride astride a miniature horse or to step into a miniature vehicle. A little later, when they have realized these impossibilities for themselves, they may still attempt to place disproportionately large dolls or teddy bears in much smaller prams or trucks.

Increasing sensitivity to the implications of this type of play, not only with regard to language development but also to the acquisition of concepts of space and time, prompted me to study the normal stages of spontaneous play of young children with simply furnished dolls' houses and toy villages. (I had found that toy farms and Noah's arks which delight somewhat older children were too confusing for under-fives.) Certain well-defined sequences became apparent, ranging from the fetching to mother in 'give and take' play at about 18 months, to the combination of highly imaginative make-believe play, with forward planning and practical application of skills like cutting out and sewing, evident at 6 or 7 years. These sequences are further illustrated and summarized in Section 4.

Constant sympathetic, but non-stressful adult encouragement to engage in every sort of spontaneous play is essential not only to the contentment but to the fundamental learning of children between one and two years of age, in whom the central nervous system is still rapidly growing and maturing in neurological structure and psychological function. From his use of playthings which he grasps, bangs, pokes, throws, holds, carries, delicately manipulates and finally

45

2 years Girl. Imitative role play developing into inventive make-believe.

46

21 months Girl. The beginnings of clearly representative play with miniature toys.

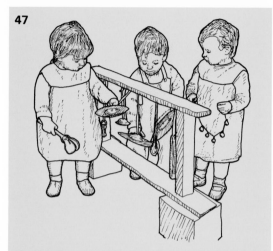

47

1¾–2¼ years Children in a day nursery playing with 'musical instruments. An interesting, if cacophonous example of solo play in close proximity.

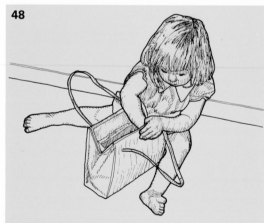

48

2½ years Girl. Handbags provide endless opportunities for exploration, manipulation, imitation – and danger.

49

2¼ years Girl. Threading beads never fails to engage interest once the fingers have acquired sufficient skill.

incorporates into make-believe play, a child first discovers through his visual, auditory and tactile perceptions what they are and what special properties they possess (i.e. their special *quality*) then he goes on to learn what he can *do* with them (i.e. their special *function*) and finally how he can adapt them to his own requirements, constructional or make-believe (their *potentialities*).

From 15–18 months onwards a child also becomes increasingly interested in picture books, first to recognize and name people, animals and objects, and familiar actions (like eating or drinking, getting into a car, posting a letter). Soon he can follow a simple story read aloud to him while he looks at the pictures. Next he begins to make comments and

ask questions. Some of this love of books and stories, which is very beneficial to his language development, is associated with his continued need for close proximity to his mother or other familiar caregivers of whom he remains strongly possessive. He is still incapable of such abstract concepts as sharing or taking turns.

He is a law unto himself, strongly resenting any infringement upon what he considers to be his constitutional rights and which he defends with vigour and determination. He has yet to develop consideration for others, especially for age-peers and children younger and more helpless than himself. This is neither 'jealousy' nor 'aggression' in the adult sense. It is a normal phase of socialization. We do not expect a child to run before he can walk. The acquisition of ability to record things and events from another person's perspective, like all primary learning processes, necessitates a certain measure of neurological maturation, appropriate experience and consistent understanding mother teaching.

2 to 3 Years

From the age of 2 years a child becomes increasingly skilful in every form of *motor activity*. He lifts and carries, climbs, leaps and runs. He can ride his tricycle forwards, using the pedals and steer it round corners. He kicks, throws and catches balls, albeit rather clumsily, but with ever-growing efficiency. (The usual stages are summarized in Section 4).

His manipulations and constructive skills steadily improve. He builds a tower of 8–10 blocks. He holds a pencil halfway down the shaft or near the point, scribbling or imitating to and fro lines and circles on a sheet of paper, or, with chalks or brush on an easel-held board, covering large areas with colour. He enjoys simple jigsaw puzzles. He can match 4 or 5 colours and several shapes, including a few simple block-capital letters, but usually cannot yet name or copy any of these. He should never be pressed to remember letters at this stage, although occasionally a particularly interested child may draw one or two and is delighted to show off his accomplishments.

He now appreciates many of the standard 'educational' toys such as formboards, nesting beakers, posting boxes, screw toys, rings on sticks, pegmen in roundabouts etc, but the more traditional playthings like dolls, teddy bears, blocks, balls, wheeled toys and domestic objects remain favourites and

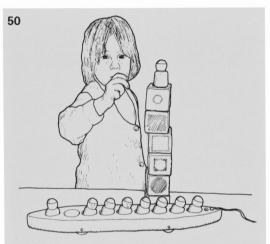

50

2½ years Two 'educational toys' employed for inventive make-believe play. She is explaining that the pegman is at the top of the lighthouse.

51

2½ years Boy painting at Granny's dining table. He is indifferent to the fact that the pictures are upside down.

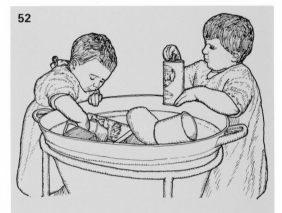

52

2½ and 3½ Boys. Water play in a nursery school, providing an excellent example of solo play in close proximity. Each child has his own playthings and playspace.

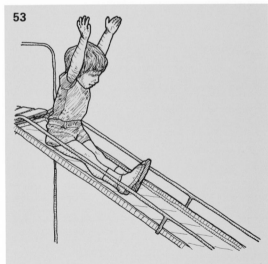

53

3½ years Boy. Gymnastics on the playground slide.

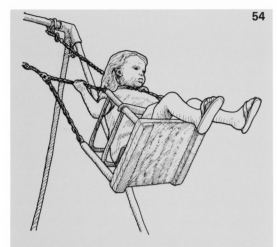

3 years Her expression is full of wonder at the changing appearance of the world beneath as she literally floats on air.

3 years Boy. The miraculous birth, appearance and behaviour of bubbles.

figure ever more prominently in both practice and pretend plays.

He instinctively uses a lively form of 'total communication' composed sometimes separately but more often simultaneously of words, gestures, mime and occasionally things as language codemes. These developments are immediately reflected in his play. He still follows familiar adults around the house, imitating and joining in their domestic activities, calling attention to his efforts, demanding approval, and asking innumerable questions. Extending earlier role play, he invents little make-believe domestic situations such as sweeping floors, baby-caring, cooking, making beds, serving meals, delivering the milk or mail, which become increasingly organized and prolonged, and which he 'plays out' with high seriousness. During these mini-dramas he talks aloud to himself, in appropriate terms, describing and explaining what he is doing, instructing himself with regard to his immediately forthcoming actions or formulating his uncertainties. Later he extends his inventions, adding some relevant dialogue to his role-play as milkman, postman, grocer or policeman. He indicates the beginnings of forward planning, such as collecting suitable items for a dolls' teaparty, or materials to construct and drive a make-believe car.

After 2½ years his moveable 'self-space' remains chiefly relative to himself and his caregivers, but he is now prepared to admit one or two familiar children briefly into his play-world and to venture intermittently into theirs. Although they play in close proximity however, the play itself is mainly of 'solo' type so that each child needs his own set of playthings and his own bit of 'territory' Collectives of more than 2 or 3 children of similar age and consequently in the same stage of immature social development, particularly if they are not well-known to each other, are seldom successful. Since ability to communicate is limited, and need to share adult attentions and playthings is not yet sufficiently understood, relationships with age-peers are unstable so that disputes are likely to be frequent and turbulent. At this developmental stage a child seems to realize his physical separateness before he appreciates his cognitive and affective individuality. For some time therefore, he remains convinced that his mother automatically apprehends what he is feeling, needing and intending. Apparently, however, under 3 years or so, he does not expect other children to share the inner workings of his mind but just assumes his own right to exercise dictatorship. Hence, in his view, a desired toy only happens to be attached to another child. The living child who holds on to 'his' toy is of little consequence. This is one of several reasons why I have come to consider that although children of 2–2½ years differ widely in social understanding, the stresses of admission to ordinary playgroups and nursery schools, without the constant availability of very familiar adult caregivers, are too burdensome for many children under 3 years of age.

3 and 4 Years

From 3 years onwards most children are ready to enjoy and profit from regular attendance at a local playgroup or nursery school. These usually provide, under trained guidance, a wealth of opportunity for developing through play the competence in everyday skills and ability to communicate effectively with other people which are the keystones of independence as persons and acceptability as personalities.

At 3 years children still need to play and therefore to learn in small groups, closely attached to one or two familiar adults. During the next year they make rapid strides in socialization, widening their circle of playmates and making less

demand for constant attention from members of staff, secure in the knowledge that this is always available when needed. By 4–4½ years they may be expected to engage amicably in all sorts of self-directed play activities with 4 to 6 age-peers. At this stage, outdoor improvised constructional building, indoor table and floor games, dressing up and make-believe play are greatly favoured. These plays are usually elaborated and carried on from day to day, manifesting an ever-increasing appreciation of the necessity for discussion, planning, sharing, taking turns and recognition of agreed rules.

From 3 years with growing command over limbs and trunk and gradual change of shape from toddler chubbiness to school-age slenderness, a child's movements begin to assume that precision, economy and grace of movement which characterizes mature control. He runs freely, climbs over and about the usual nursery apparatus, negotiates slides, crawls through barrels and jumps on small trampolines. He walks up and down stairs, one foot to a step, without needing to hold on to a rail, although he is glad to have one of suitable height available. He is able to jump down from ever-increasing heights keeping both feet together and landing without falling. He

56

3½ years Boy. Simple insert jigsaws retain their fascination for much longer than one expects.

57

3 years Girl recently admitted to nursery school, is still a shy onlooker. Her reversion to an earlier immature posture and grasp of doll clearly demonstrate her present feelings of insecurity.

58 **3 years** Girl, supremely secure, engaging in elaborate role and make-believe play.

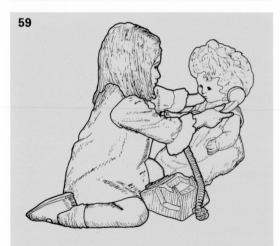

59 She invents both participants in the dialogue, using different tones of voice and choice of words.

60 **3½ years** (same boy as Fig. 56). He is well able to cope with this more complicated jigsaw puzzle, although its large size necessitated frequent unhurried contemplation.

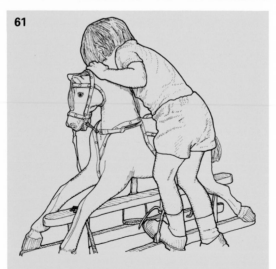

61 **3½ years** Boy gracefully mounting a large, old rocking horse, greatly beloved by all child visitors.

rides a tricycle confidently using the pedals and steering safely round sharp corners.

He now has a clear appreciation of space in relation to his own body in size and shape, at rest and in movement. He has discovered from experience the spaces where he can pass himself and those which he can navigate with large wheeled toys such as trucks, dolls' prams and pedal cars, steering forwards, sideways and backwards. He carries large blocks, planks and boards and with the help of co-operative playmates builds houses, cars, space ships, shops, hospitals and other structures in which to conduct a host of vivid make-believe activities.

Hand skills are also rapidly improving through play with small toys like blocks, jigsaw puzzles, miniature cars, dolls' houses etc. Both boys and girls enjoy pencil work and cutting out shapes with scissors. From threading of large beads on bootlaces, then smaller beads on thinner strings they proceed finally to real sewing and knitting. Girls usually learn more quickly than boys to put their needlework skills to practical use, making something for their dolls to wear or for use in their domestic make-believe plays.

Block building remains popular for

many years, proceeding from the simple stereotypes of trains, towers and bridges still employed in most pre-school psychological tests, to highly complicated structures ingeniously planned and carefully executed. Incidentally, I have often wondered if earnest examiners, who have not had my advantages for fringe observation and interested eavesdropping, have any idea how much success in performance on these tests may be due to practice and even coaching at home from adults and older children. I have long since preferred to evaluate them in terms of *how* they are carried out, which is very much more enlightening. Children of both sexes first employ blocks purely as manipulative objects, then through imitation, copying and instruction, gradually extend their forward programming or 'blue-printing' to the construction of structures which (like their spontaneous drawings) they name beforehand. Later these constructions are often taken into other, more complicated and fanciful play with miniature cars, furniture and dolls to form part of the settings for domestic happenings and street scenes. These sequences are further discussed in Section 3.

Jig-saw puzzles provide much fun and interest from about $2\frac{1}{2}$ years onwards

62

Same boy. Active play merges into make-believe. This is show-jumping in its fullest competitive splendour.

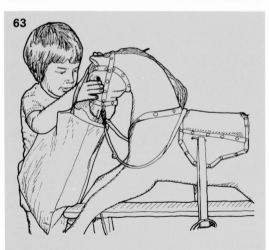

63

Same boy. After the trials, the successful horse is fondly fed from mother's shopping bag.

64

$2\frac{1}{2}$–4 years   Children enjoying active play in the park, while their mothers, sitting nearby, chatting to each other, keep watch.

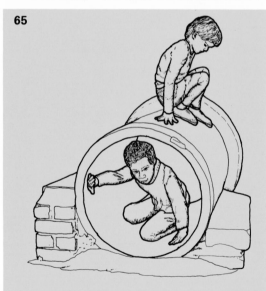

65

Young children in an adventure playground, demonstrating several interesting aspects of activity play.

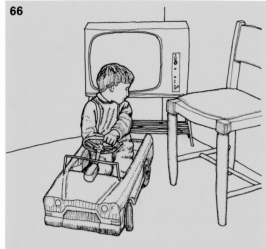

3½ years Boy demonstrating skilful motor control and excellent spatial sense.

Girl **2 years** and boy **5 years** Blissfully content in a quiet half hour at home with mother.

although even younger children may enjoy placing shapes in simple form-boards and shaped blocks in post-boxes, provided they are not unduly pressed to 'perform' correctly. Suitable first jigsaws are those in which single coloured pictures of some familiar objects are placed in separate matching spaces in a large wooden frame. From 3 years onwards puzzles with a greater number of places are needed. It is noticeable that many children of this age are more interested in analytic fitting together of the shapes than building up the picture, so that they will construct it from the plain wooden back without regard for the attractively coloured and designed front. Later assembly of a picture with many more pieces becomes all-important. It is not clear why some children perform in this fashion, but it may be that they are manifesting the commonly found sequence of learning which proceeds from general overview through separate analysis of details to final immediate synthesis into a well apprehended whole.

Play with plasticine and other mouldable materials including the use of real dough in real cooking, is much enjoyed from 3 years onwards, and particularly with over-4s. It remains an attractive indoor pastime for many years.

Spontaneous drawings of 3s and 4s (as distinct from copy-design which like writing is not discussed here) become increasingly elaborate and diverse in colour, form and content although still remaining chiefly concerned with people, houses, transport-vehicles and flowers. At first most of these paintings employ only one colour. It is frequently disconcerting to a parent who has carefully provided a selection of brightly coloured paints or crayons to see their child nonchalantly mixing all the lovely clear pigments together into a mud-coloured monochrome and then painting with that, or randomly choosing one crayon with disregard for all the others. Soon the charm and appropriateness of colour in relation to whatever visual image the child has in mind delights him. At first the 3-year-old does not name his drawing until he has finished. It is not until about four years that he announces beforehand what he is about to draw indicating that he has some sort of preliminary 'blue-print' in his head before he begins. These sequences are also further discussed in Section 3.

Interest in music-making usually in the form of percussion instruments or simple wind instruments usually begins to show itself from about 3½ to 4 years. Children with exceptional musical talent nearly always manifest unusually sophisticated tastes very early, not only in their listening, but also in expression, recognizing and recalling tunes learned from adults and older children, or heard on radio or record. Some may ask for and even manage to play such musical instruments as are within their capacity to manipulate. These children, like all other gifted children deserve every encouragement, but should never be unduly pressed. Proud, affectionate parents of precocious children are particularly open to such insidious temptations.

Meanwhile, between 3 and 4 years a child's ability to use spoken language rapidly improves both in vocabulary and syntax so that, in spite of residual infantile mis-pronunciations and grammatical errors, his speech is generally intelligible even to people outside his immediate family. He and his playmates informally communicating in a glorious mixture of words, exaggerated vocal cadences, facial expressions and telling gestures, understand each other perfectly.

By 4 years verbal interchanges of every sort, friendly, informative, questioning, argumentative, explanatory and instructive become increasingly evident in all aspects of play, especially in make-believe situations. Once free communication has been established within any group, the signs of leadership show up clearly, the dominant child deciding who shall play the major roles such as father, mother, shop-keeper, bus conductor, hospital doctor etc., and who shall be the subsidiary characters. The leader may or may not generously agree to later interchanges of roles and taking turns. Adult observers can only marvel at the group's meticulous observance of these roles and rules which are mainly unformulated but crystal clear to the players. Non-conformers are soon tacitly eliminated. At this stage a child's make-believe, subjective world is so vivid to him that he is sometimes very hazy concerning what is fact and what is fiction so that inexperienced caregivers may be startled by his apparently blatant disregard for objective truth. Having simultaneously found their tongues and a broad sense of humour, four-year-olds delight in rhymes, riddles, simple jokes and verbal teasing. They love having stories read to them, especially when they can simultaneously look at illustrations. They greatly enjoy Punch and Judy and other puppet shows, including the admirable children's programmes on television and often are seen acting them out personally later. Some children have become so sensitive to the potentialities of story books that they clamour to be

68

Girl **3½ years** and boy **3 years**   Making small plasticine models of domestic and other objects.

69

Girl **5½ years** with boy **3½ years**   She copes effectively with a very complicated jigsaw, carefully explaining her strategies.

70

4½ years Handed a box of miniature toys, she scrutinizes the collection *in situ*, before selecting items for assembly. A younger child would probably first spread them all out on the table top.

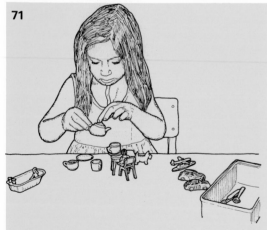

71

A few minutes later, assembly is almost complete – domestic items together, bath 'upstairs' and items of transport 'outside'.

72

Boy **3½ years**, girl **5 years** Elaborate make-believe play in the Wendy House.

73

Same children in borrowed costumes, engaged in a classic game of cowboys and Indians. The girl was naturally assigned the less active role.

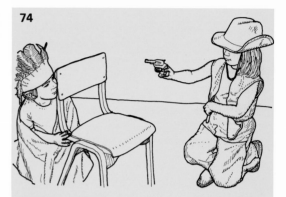

74

But after a few minutes having taken off all his cowboy costume, he insists on a change of role – with his sister's gracious agreement.

taught to read themselves but this needs to be approached cautiously. Although they now need age-peers to play with, they still enjoy being with their parents and siblings at home, continuing to learn by imitating, trying out new skills, listening, talking and asking endless questions. They particularly like having some special job of their own to do, provided it is not too heavy or too tediously pressed.

By this time they can mentally detach the physical aspects of 'self' from those of 'non-self' sufficiently well to be able to envisage the situation of hills, houses, bridges and other prominent features in the landscape from another's position in space, and they can appreciate some of the implications of visual perspective, although this does not yet appear in their drawings. They also begin to demonstrate a growing sense of compassion and responsibility. Whereas formerly they appeared to be content to remain detached observers of a playmate's hurt or distress, they now show attentive sympathy, running to seek adult help or offering comfort in personal contact or soothing words. They are helpful and protective, albeit somewhat bossy, towards younger children, particularly their own siblings. They show great fondness for family pets and like to include them in their make-believe activities.

Appetite for adventure is not always matched by appreciation of the dangers of road traffic, swimming pools and playground equipment, particularly with boys, who seem to benefit less than girls do from verbal appeals, prohibitions and explanations. It is not clear whether this almost universal characteristic is due to the boy's greater courage or to his lesser maturity of foresight, but in relation to learning about accident prevention 'discovery methods' of education are totally inappropriate.

5 and 6 Years

From this stage onwards a child continues steadily to develop his everyday competence and his powers of communication. In his play he shows an increasing enjoyment not only of elaborate make-believe activities, but also for complicated indoor and outdoor games which require knowledgeable preliminary instruction, hard practice, strict adherence to rules and a sense of fair play. His personal aptitudes for sports, crafts and the creative arts become ever more apparent in his selective use of leisure time, his choice of companions and the games they play whether at home, in playgrounds with special equipment, or in open fields and narrow streets with no

75

4½ years   Boy. Coloured plastic shapes provide excellent opportunities for inventive picture-making and conversation.

76

4½ and 5 years   Attending a playgroup, these boys collaborate in constructing a very elaborate street scene complete with church, high-rise flats, flyover and traffic.

77

4½ years Cutting out a carpet for her dolls' house.

78

5 years She has just learned how to knit and is happily practising her new skill.

79

Children in the paddling pool of a neighbouring park. Their mothers, seated together close by, were keeping a watchful eye on their activities.

80

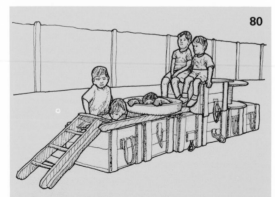

3–5 years Children attending a day nursery. This elaborate construction, assembled and dismantled every day, provides opportunity for every kind of outdoor play.

81

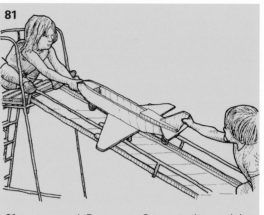

3½ years and **5 years** Co-operative activity play on the slide.

82

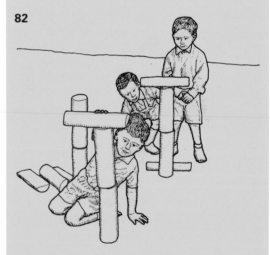

4 years Elaborate building with large wooden blocks involving considerable forward planning and precise construction.

equipment at all other than the chants and rituals of long unwritten tradition, coupled with lively contemporary improvisations.

For the next few years the separate interests of boys and girls are clearly evident in their spontaneous play, although in school playgrounds their teachers usually organize and encourage mixed play activities.

At School

Even for children who have previously attended playgroups or nursery school the abrupt transition to ordinary school must be at least as potentially stressful as the much more frequently discussed transition in adolescence from the certainties of school to the uncertainties of open employment. As a paediatrician, I can only consider it regrettable that modern conditions do not allow, let alone encourage, half-time attendance for a term or two so that children who need it may be accorded a period of more gentle introduction to the large spaces, overwhelming noise and bustle and the wide liberty of occupational choice which, for some children, lead to confusion rather than curiosity and insecurity rather than independence. Those robust characters who can take all

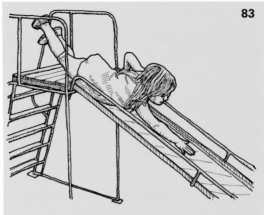

83

5 years   Girl on slide – compare with same posture of baby in Fig. 14.

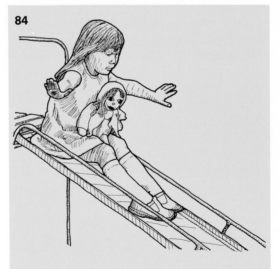

84

Same girl – gymnastics on the slide, involving appropriate verbal instruction of her doll.

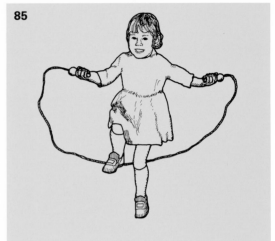

85

4 years   Learning to skip, but not yet very proficient.

86

4½ years   He is a competent performer on the trampoline.

A group of familiar friends on the roundabout in the park.

The same children performing skilfully on a more difficult roundabout (they called it 'doing Olympics').

A certain element of danger adds attraction to this swing.

A lovely silhouette of activity in the park.

these novel experiences in their stride undoubtedly possess some preliminary advantage. They now have greatly enlarged opportunities for activity and a wider circle of companions from whom to choose special friends. The bookishly inclined have a well selected library, the talkative more to relate when they go home. But less immediately forthcoming children, given the opportunity to adapt to their new environment will eventually find their own contentments. Quiet retiring children are not always immature. They are sometimes outstanding creative, the future serious thinkers and academic high-fliers, who from an early age seem instinctively to realize their need for periods of complete physical and mental repose, when they are happier alone in the book corner than in the playground with their more boisterous age-peers.

Section 3

OUTLINES OF PARTICULAR PLAY SEQUENCES

Cup

92

9 months Grasping the cup right side up with both hands he brings the rim to his mouth, looking at his caregiver.

94

12 months The foregoing imitation reminds her of the true function of cups and spoons and she promptly offers a clear example of definition-by-use.

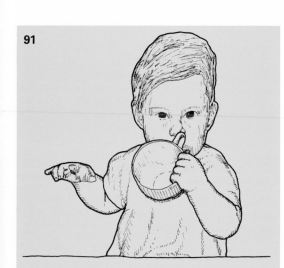

91

6 months Having grasped with both hands, she passes to one hand and brings the most prominent feature of the cup to her mouth.

93

12 months Having just observed me place cup and spoon on table after testing her hearing by stroking the rim of this cup, she seizes the cup and spoon and successfully imitates.

95

2¼ years Cups, spoons and other related domestic items are happily incorporated into make-believe play.

Hand Bell

Rung by adult while child watched, and then presented upright on table top.

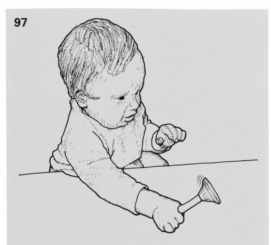

97

9 months Grasps midhandle with one hand and delightedly bangs noisily and repeatedly on table top.

96

24 weeks Grasps bell at base with both hands, obviously concentrating serious attention on activity. Immediately afterwards he brought the top of handle to his mouth.

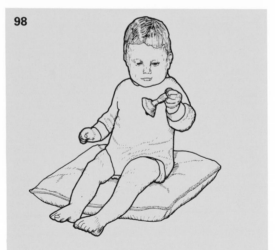

98

10 months Seizes top of handle with one hand and rings bell enjoying musical sound.

99

11 months Pokes at clapper with index finger.

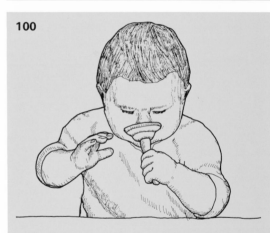

100

12 months The bell shape reminds him of a cup and he acts accordingly. It is difficult to decide whether this is fortuitous exploration or deferred definition-by-use.

Block Play

101

9 months Holding a block competently in each hand, she brings them together in interested comparison. A few moments later she found considerable pleasure in clicking them together.

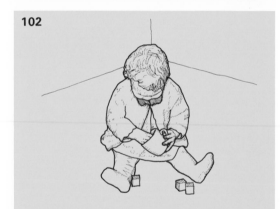

102

12 months Having found a block hidden under the cup, she begins to explore some further possibilities on her own account.

103

15 months Having arranged these blocks as shown entirely by himself, he is apparently recalling some previous game of 'pushing a train' with an older playmate.

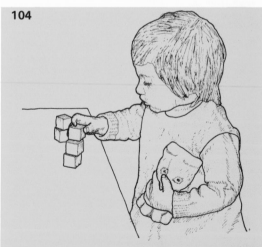

104

15 months She has always enjoyed handling blocks and readily builds little towers of 2 and 3 with her R. hand while grasping a larger stuffed animal toy with the other.

105

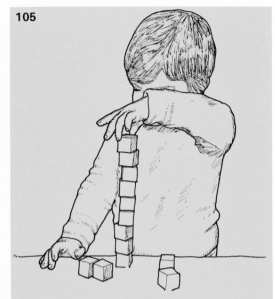

2 years A particularly competent young architect. Having built half the tower with his right hand, he shifted attention to the left. This interesting form of self-training is very common.

106

3 years She is giving a lovely example of previous learning. Before it was possible to provide a model bridge, she used up every block in sight and is counting them aloud.

107

3½ years Another very competent young boy. His mother is building 3 steps behind a screen – a difficult 'test' at this age.

108

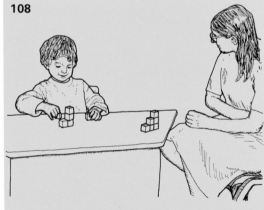

But he has long experience of constructive block play and has no difficulty in copying the model.

109

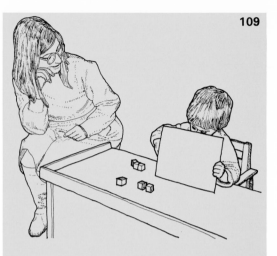

Like most intelligent children he delights in sharing his expertise. Having seized the screen he builds behind it.

110

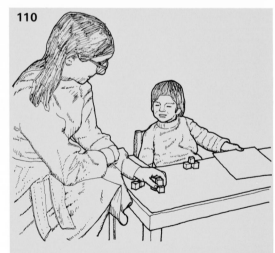

He is saying 'Mummy do it'. It is interesting to note that he chose another block construction for her to copy. (This whole sequence of events was entirely spontaneous.)

Artistic Performance

111

12 months Girl. Imitative artist at work. Typical grasp of pencil at its proximal end with R. hand with 'mirror' posturing in L. hand. A moment later she passed the pencil from R. to L. again marking paper.

112

15 months Boy. Firmer grasp of the pencil lower down the shaft, and improved end-product of to and fro lines and dots. Mirror posture in L. hand.

113

21 months Girl. Larger brush work at an easel. Her productions are still more in the nature of visuomotor activities than in representative pictures.

114

3½ years Boy. Interesting example of simultaneous two-handed performance. The pencil grip near tip is more mature, but the production is still non-pictorial.

115

3½ years Girl. R. handed mature grip of pencil with non-engagement of L. She asked to be given a letter to copy. She did not seem to realize hers was upside down.

116

4 years Girl. Drawing a typical age-characteristic house with cornered windows, simultaneously thinking aloud about it. The mature grip of R. hand and the helpful use of L. to steady the paper are well shown.

117

Boy **3½ years** and girl **4 years** painting human figures. The boy used only black paint, the girl several colours. The end-products are both fairly age-characteristic. Originally reported these as self-portraits, but cheerfully admitted many inaccuracies.

118

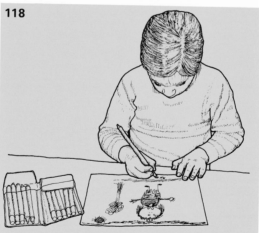

4¾ years Girl producing a colourful self-portrait with numerous common environmental embellishments — yellow sun, narrow blue sky, green trees, brown earth. She is printing her name beneath. She works briskly and silently in happy concentration.

Play with Dolls' Houses and Model Villages

119

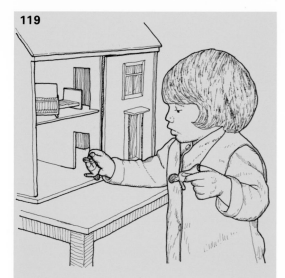

15 months Boy. Miniature toys are merely small items to be manipulated and put in and out of an upright box-like container.

120

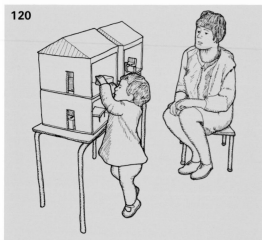

18 months Girl. The miniature toys are objects for give-and-take play with mother.

121

Same child — mother names toys and child repeats name, but still does not appreciate that the toys represent real-life objects.

122

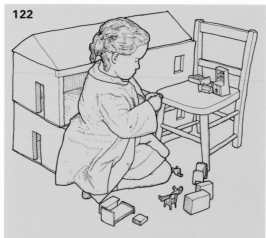

2½ years She knows that the toys are representative, but prefers to assemble them in smaller, separated groups outside the dolls' house.

123

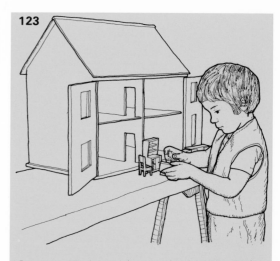

3 years This boy also assembles meaningful groups, near to but outside the dolls' house, talking to himself continuously meanwhile.

124

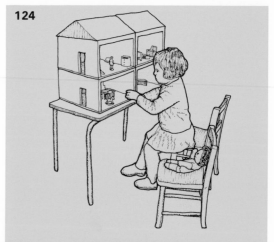

3¼ years Having placed her large doll protectively beside her, she plays with the miniatures inside one room of the house, carrying on a long, audible monologue to herself and the large doll.

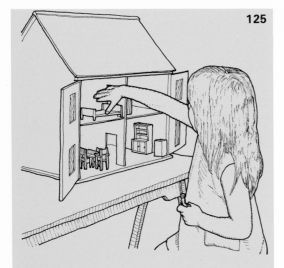

5 years   Girl playing constructively all over the house. Although silent, her thoughts are busily engaged.

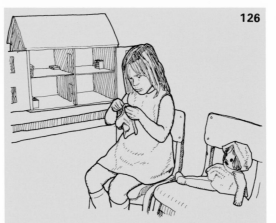

She had recently learned to sew and having conducted a spring clean, makes curtains for the windows. Incidentally, like the younger child in Fig. 124, she has seated her large doll close by with loving care.

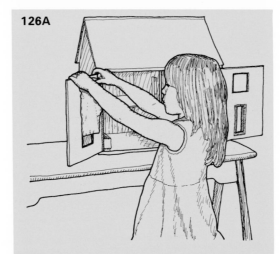

The half-made curtains are measured against the windows.

6 and 6½ years   Girls — 'special friends' they said, engaged in elaborate co-operative make-believe play in the dolls' house. The play goes on continuously from day to day. They had papered the walls and made all the soft furnishings.

128

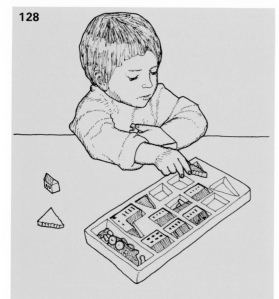

21 months Boy. Presented with this boxed model village, he named the houses and trees but did not group them, preferring to treat the items as an inset jigsaw puzzle. He was most competent at this.

129

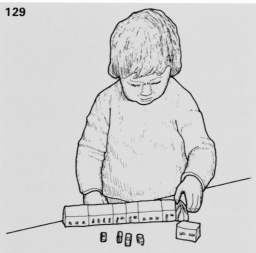

3 years She aligned all the houses in one neat row, and the cars in another row, telling herself aloud which member of the family lived in each house.

131

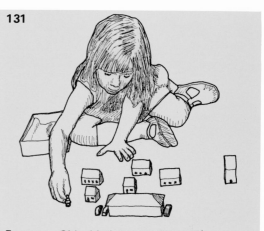

5 years Girl with the same village. The railway station is behind the houses, which are more regularly placed 'with their own gardens'. The cars are at the station awaiting the commuters' return home.

130

3½ years Boy. The railway station occupies the most prominent situation in the centre of his array. Houses were scattered haphazardly, but cars and aeroplanes occupied strategic positions and were freely moved.

132

6½ years Girl. Her village is at the same time more artistically and more realistically arranged. Her younger brother engaged in play of his own, insisted upon the inclusion of his 'jumbo-jet', and she allowed it to land in a nearby field.

Ball Play

18 months Boy. Still too uncertain of his legs to stand on one foot, he just walks into a large ball without ability to kick it.

2 years Although still unable to kick the ball, she steadily raises her arms to balancing position and lifts one foot momentarily, without the desired result.

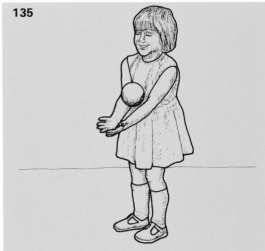

3½ years Although able to kick a large ball gently she is still unable to co-ordinate eyes, arms and hands to catch a ball. Her whole posture is age-typical of girls.

3½ years Boys are much more capable. The head, body-posture and anticipatory position of legs, arms and hands is age-characteristic of boys.

137

But he is less skilful in catching a smaller ball approaching more rapidly.

138

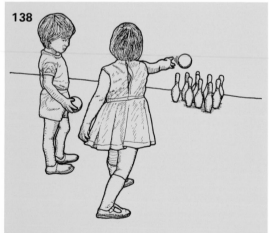

The same children playing skittles. The girl's throwing posture is well shown.

139

And the boy's much more effective performance – his whole body actively engaged.

140

4½ years Boy's running approach to a kick. His entire attention is harmoniously concentrated.

141

Same boy throwing a small ball, eyes focused on the objective.

142

5¼ years Boy batting incoming ball. The typical posture and visual fixation are well shown. The bowler is out of sight. The younger boy of **3½ years** who is fielding is also learning about the rules of the game.

Outline of Expected Ages and Stages in the Development of Spoken Language*

* Taken from the *Manual to the Stycar Language Test*, published by NFER Publishing Company, 1976. © Mary D. Sheridan, 1976.

Ages	Manifestations	Stages
4½ months	Reception	Localises and pays obvious interested attention to close-by meaningful sounds, particularly familiar voices.
	Expression	Vocalizes responsively when spoken to face-to-face: chuckles and squeals. Babbles to self and others using sing-song intonation and single or double 'syllables'. Cries loudly when hungry, annoyed, bored or uncomfortable.
7 months	Reception	Immediately attends to and localizes nearby everyday meaningful sounds, particularly human voices. Beginning to respond discriminatively to emotional overtones in speech of familiar adults (i.e. soothing, prohibitive etc.).
	Expression	Babbles continuously to self and others in long, tuneful repetitive strings of syllables with wide range of pitch, combining open vowels and (usually) single consonant sounds. Beginning to imitate adults' playful vocalizations in face-to-face situations.
14 months	Reception	Responds appropriately to quiet meaningful everyday sounds within 3 or 4 metres. Recognizes own and family names and words for several common objects and activities. Sensitive to expressive cadences in speech of familiars.
	Expression	Jabbers continuously to self and others employing loud, prosodic tuneful jargon. Emergence of first single words used correctly, consistently and spontaneously (i.e. not imitatively) but usually comprehensible, even to familiars, only in situational context. Ekes out articulatory difficulties with urgent intonations and finger pointings.
21 months	Reception	Shows clearly by correct response to spoken communications that he hears and understands many more words than he can utter.
	Expression	Speaks 20–50+ single words and is beginning to join 2 or 3 words in meaningful sentences of agent-action-object type. Refers to self by name. Owing to numerous infantilisms speech sometimes unintelligible to familiars and almost always to strangers. Echoes final or stressed word in sentences addressed to him. Shows brief imitative role play alone or with friendly adult. Beginning to play meaningfully with miniature toys.

Ages	Manifestations	Stages
3 years	Reception	Comprehends literal meanings of words and beginning to appreciate common semantic variations.
	Expression	Echolalia persists. Vocabulary rapidly enlarging. Uses sentences of 3–5 words, personal pronouns and most prepositions. Talks continuously to self at play. Infantilisms of articulation and grammar gradually diminishing. Intelligible even to strangers. Asks many questions of Who? What? Where? type. Engages in simple make-believe play alone or with one or two others. Plays meaningfully with miniature toys providing simultaneous running commentary.
$4\frac{1}{2}$ years	Reception	Competent for most everyday situations provided sentences are not longer than 6–7 words and vocabulary employed reflects child's experience.
	Expression	Uses large vocabulary with conventional grammar and syntax. Articulation still shows residual infantilisms chiefly involving r-l-w-y, t-k, and s-f-th consonant groups, but speech (usually) intelligible even to strangers. Narrates long stories. Asks numerous questions of When? Why? How? type and meanings of words. Engages in elaborate make-believe play with groups of 3–6 peers. Draws 'pictures' (usually) of people, houses, transport and flowers.
$6\frac{1}{2}$ years	Reception	Completely competent for all home, school and neighbourhood situations.
	Expression	Spoken language fully intelligible, grammatical and fluent. Engages in elaborate make-believe play and win/lose team games with chosen friends, explaining rules and objectives lucidly. Draws more elaborate 'pictures' showing people and objects in all sorts of everyday situations. Interested in learning to read, write and calculate.

THE PLAY OF HANDICAPPED CHILDREN

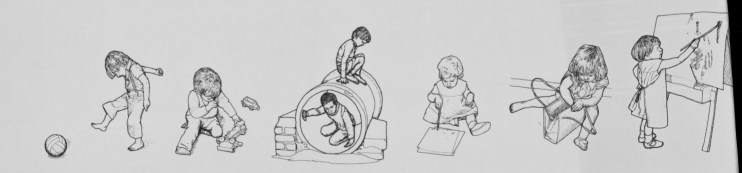

In order to discuss the spontaneous play of handicapped children and how it can assist their optimum development, it is necessary first to explain my use of the term 'normal'.

Unfortunately, in the context of child development, the word is applied in at least three different ways according to professional bias. To some authorities a 'normal child' is an ideal creature seldom (if ever) encountered in real life, superbly healthy, highly intelligent, personally attractive and socially competent. Other authorities consider a normal child to be one who has achieved an average score or 'norm' on some standardized developmental scale. Field-working paediatricians, teachers, parents and even more particularly grandparents, know that the range of normality is wide with limits which are very difficult to define. Fortunately, however, to experienced observers, deviant and borderline manifestations become ever-increasingly easier to recognize. I would therefore define a normal child as one whose growth and development correspond with what may be reasonably expected in eight out of ten of his age-peers. (Of the remaining 2 in 10, some will be more advanced and others more retarded than their age-peers.)

There is general agreement that all early learning is related to increasingly effective integration of sensory and motor experience. These learning experiences are themselves the result of imitation and constant practice of well-established adult usages. Consequently, children with any serious defect of vision, hearing, locomotor equipment, or central nervous system functioning, which interferes with the normal organization of sensory intake and motor output, are at a disadvantage compared with their normal age-peers in gathering a working knowledge of the ordinary world. For this reason they must be encouraged to make best use of whatever *assets* they possess, while at the same time ensuring that they persevere with activities designed to reverse or mitigate the effects of their *disabilities*. Hence, in planning any remedial programme, it is first necessary to obtain comprehensive paediatric and psychological assessment, with full, friendly personal exchange of information between parents, therapists and teachers.

As noted in previous sections, young *normal children* in all their playtime engagements, are eager learners, showing strong drive and concentration. They have a compelling urge to know and to do. Having mastered any basic skill they spontaneously press forward, devising additional complexities and difficulties in task performance and then working hard to overcome them. When they recognize the need for knowledgeable outside assistance, they actively seek it.

In contrast to their normal age-peers, *handicapped children* of all types, excepting those who happen to be blessed with good intelligence and high motivation, are slow learners, lacking in drive and powers of concentration. Having achieved a basic skill they tend, unless continually encouraged towards new goals, to perseverate indefinitely or gradually to relax and regress. They seldom appreciate the necessity to seek outside help, but just give up trying. In order to progress, they require patient individual, step-by-step instruction and must be gently but firmly stimulated to constant practice. In short they must be given prolonged 'mother-teaching at mother-distance'.

Even seemingly unpromising handicapped children, by reason of biological maturational factors alone, may be expected to manifest some forward progression, although their developmental gains will probably be uneven, fluctuating and dissociated. Physically handicapped children with normal intelligence and stable personality often show a rewardingly rapid response to appropriate therapies, devoting to the attainment and practice of gross motor skills, hand-eye coordination and interpersonal communication (though not always in spoken words), exceptional powers of concentration and perseverance. Instinctive biological drives, however, can only take the most strongly motivated children a certain distance. Owing to their limited opportunity for exploration and exploitation of their environment in the early years of life, all subsequent developmental stages tend to be delayed, prolonged and tethered to practical objectives. Unlike their normal contemporaries they cannot automatically acquire that store of common knowledge and social understanding which enables ordinary children of three years and upwards to fit contentedly into and obtain full benefit from admission to a playgroup or nursery school. Consequently, parents of handicapped children need to be given not only kindly sympathy, but knowledgeable guidance regarding the developmental progressions in learning from play which normal children take in their stride, and the provisions which must be made at every stage.

It is convenient to discuss these provisions under the headings used in the previous section. I make no excuse for emphasizing several matters about which I feel very strongly.

Playthings and Play Equipment

In well-intentioned efforts to encourage 'sense-training' and 'concept-formation', a handicapped child is often almost exclusively provided with 'abstract' play materials: such as screw-toys, nesting boxes, geometrically shaped blocks, pegboards, counting frames etc. 'Educational' toys of this sort undoubtedly assist manipulative skills and memory for number, colour and form, but because they provide little opportunity for extending a child's everyday vocabulary, his social understanding or his creative make-believe play, they must be used with discretion. Hence, from long experience, I would stress my conviction that all the well-tried traditional playthings such as rattles, balls, blocks, dolls, wheeled toys and everyday household objects, from which normal children derive so much pleasure and profit, are of primary and not secondary importance in the natural, happy, fundamental learning of handicapped children.

A few soft toys are generally acceptable, although in the earliest stages, they provide little active stimulation except for holding and throwing, and sometimes as the 'transitional objects' beloved by most normal children (Ekecrantz and Rudhe, 1972), but they come into their own later in make-believe play. Expensive clockwork and other 'finished' commercial toys are seldom desirable.

There is no need to stress the importance of ensuring that all playthings are washable and flameproof, impossible to swallow, safe to handle, suck and throw.

Playspace

The same comment already made regarding the needs of normal children for a 'personal territory' and for adequate free-ranging spaces in and out of doors, applies with equal pertinence to handicapped children. Indoor playrooms must be clean, warm and safe as well as suitably equipped.

The use of common outdoor *playground equipment* should be encouraged, provided reasonable safety precautions are taken and adequate supervision is available. Handicapped children of all ages enjoy active play which is within their physical capacity. They should therefore be given suitable opportunities for play with trucks, tricycles, pedal cars, climbing frames, slides, trampolines, swings, see-saws, sandpits, paddling-pools and boating ponds. Their sensible use promotes mobility, self-reliance and good comradeship.

Playtime

Many house-bound handicapped children have too much time to spare with too little opportunity to engage in rewarding pursuits. Occupations of various sorts may be pressed upon them by well-meaning adults but they have few playmates of their own age. Consequently they become bored and unhappy. Some may persevere endlessly but unprogressively with one activity, others just drift into a state of aimless inertia or whining distress. To such children and their worried parents Toy Libraries and other specialized services (see list of references pages 85–87) have much to offer.

Playmates

Admission to a suitable playgroup or nursery school may provide happy interests for the child and welcome relief for his parents, but judgement of suitability must never be founded merely in terms of 'Can he possibly be contained in this group?' but always in terms of 'Is this particular group *good* for *him*?'. The problems of simultaneously 'individualizing' and 'normalizing' any type of nursery environment are numerous and seldom immediately obvious to the parents or even to the staff. Gradual introduction, kindly supervision and periodic evaluation of progress are therefore essential in the interest of all concerned.

SPECIAL GROUPS

Although it is not at present possible to discuss in detail the special play needs of the various types of handicapped children, a few practical notes may be helpful.

Children with Severe Physical Handicaps

This is a large group with very variable pathological conditions, some of which have existed from birth while others have been acquired as a result of disease or injury. Among the more common congenital malformations are hydrocephalus, spina bifida and deformities of arms, hands, legs or feet. Other serious disablements are the result of cerebral palsy or poliomyelitis. Some result from accidents at home and in the street. Every child presents his own unique problem for paediatricians, therapists, bio-engineers and teachers. Consequently, his early home management and later educational placement require very carful consideration. Physically handicapped children are often such rewarding pupils that there may be a danger that they will be over-pressed and allowed too little opportunity for relaxation and simple fun.

Children with mobility defects cannot explore for themselves nor follow adults round the house and learn to imitate their everyday activities. Moreover for many children with cerebral palsy, spina bifida and head injuries, normal integration and interpretation of sensory experience, which depend not only upon *intake* but also upon memory storage, may be disturbed. In these circumstances, *initiation* of pre-motor assembly i.e. sequential forward 'programming' of voluntary movements, is likely to present serious difficulty. Appropriate provisions for play can only be made in the light of observational experience.

143

4½ years Boy with congenital malformation of arms and hands happily learning to use artificial upper limbs. Intelligent and verbally advanced.

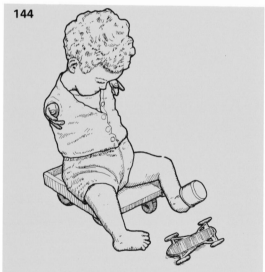

144

3 years Boy with congenital deformities of upper limbs using his feet as graspers while ambulating on his specially designed mobile platform. Later successfully fitted with artificial arms.

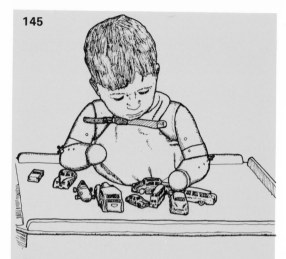

145

5 years Boy with congenital shortening of upper limbs using his first artificial arms in play with miniature toys. He chatted fluently.

146

5 years Physically handicapped boy preferring to use his own shortened limbs in skilfully constructing a jigsaw puzzle, although he could well control his artificial limbs.

147

5 years A girl with congenital deformities of the lower limbs engaged in enjoyable conversation with her nursery school teacher.

148

6 and 7 years Spastic children in a residential school, helping the kindhearted cook to make pastry on a rainy afternoon.

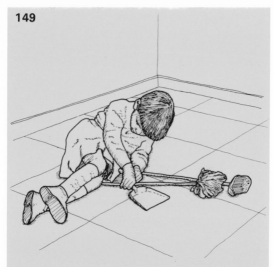

149

5 years Girl with cerebral palsy, unable to walk, engaged in domestic play. She deliberately chose these Wendy-house sized models and lying on her side, proceeded to sweep the floor.

150

6 years Girl with cerebral palsy, having dressed up appropriately, engaging in affectionate caregiving dollplay.

151

5 and 3½ years Spastic children in a Wendy House. The girl is obviously enjoying her richly conceived make-believe play. She has also taken a delicate little younger boy under affectionate protective care.

152

6 and 7 years Spastic children building with large light packing cases made of plastic foam. They later took turns crawling through the completed bridge.

Mentally Handicapped Children

These constitute the largest and most heterogeneous of all the groups of handicapped children, presenting every variety and degree of retarded development. Many have additional defects of vision and hearing which add to their intellectual difficulties but may go unnoticed in the absence of comprehensive paediatric assessment. Children with Down's syndrome (mongolism) form a major sub-group. They show general delay in all aspects of development and particularly in language acquisition. They are usually affectionate, contented and socially acceptable little children. In their play they are notably imitative and greatly benefit from kindly training and supervision, often achieving unexpected competence in everyday skills.

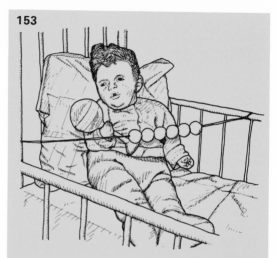

153

14 months Mentally handicapped child with multiple physical deformities. He later threw out the untethered toy he is holding and regarding, and turned attention to the chain of balls.

154

2½ years Multi-handicapped, severely retarded child, more interested in the primitive activity of hand-watching than in playing with the dolls her parents had brought her.

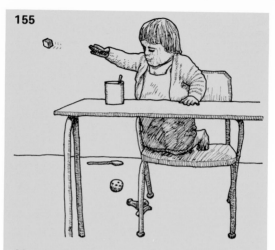

155

22 months Mentally handicapped child nonchalantly casting away playthings with little regard for their ultimate destination.

156

24 months Mentally handicapped child actively exploring her everyday world, interestedly engaged in the study of domestic objects.

157

3 years Mentally handicapped girl bathing her doll.

158

2¼ years Mentally handicapped boy demonstrating a more advanced type of imitative play, involving a toy telephone and his doll.

159

2½ and 3 years Mentally handicapped children engaged in water play, providing a good example of solo play in close proximity.

160

3 years Mentally handicapped girl looking with interest at a book. The fact that it is upside down does not seem to matter.

161

4 years Mentally handicapped boy discovering the relationship between his own size and shape and the inside volume of a large cardboard box.

162

4 years Mentally handicapped boy not yet able to co-ordinate movements of eyes and limbs in order to catch a large ball. Note the immaturity of posture.

163

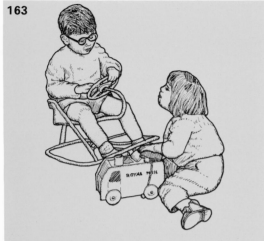

4 years Two mentally handicapped children in companionable make-believe play.

165

11 years Well grown but severely mentally handicapped girl still playing happily in the sand-tray like a much younger child.

164

4 and 6 years Two other mentally handicapped children showing good fellowship. The little boy is still manifesting a very early stage of artistic production.

Children in Hospital

A child in hospital is in very special need of playthings and playmates, appropriate to his age and disability, as well as to the unusual environmental circumstances. Although it is unwise to overcrowd his cot with too many toys as this tends to confuse him, he needs to have more than one at a time available, if he is not to become bored. If he is at the stage of throwing things out of his cot, he may use this skill frequently, in order to attract adult attention or to seek co-operation in give-and-take play. It is wise to ensure that throwable playthings are firmly tied to the cot.

Older children dislike to think that they have fallen behind their classmates when they return to school. Indeed, for most children of school age, once they have recovered from the acute phases of an illness, lessons are the most welcome form of occupational therapy. Hence the 'playlady' and the teacher are indispensable members of staff in children's wards.

166

12 months Normally intelligent baby under treatment in hospital for fracture of lower limb, throwing plaything from cot with obvious interest in direction and nature of fall. Posture typical of purposeful throw from sitting position.

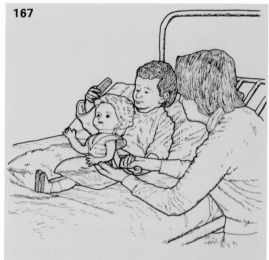

167

3½ years Child in hospital following an accident. While engaging in caregiving doll play with her right hand, she clings tightly to her mother's hand with the other—a simple touching little scene.

168

9 years This intelligent girl, obliged to spend several weeks in an orthopaedic ward, is deeply engaged in literary composition. She said happily, 'I love lessons'.

Visually Handicapped Children

This is a numerically small but seriously handicapped group. Visual disorders arise from a multitude of causes either within the eye itself or in those areas of the brain which deal with the interpretation of visual phenomena. Lacking normal opportunities to relate visually to their caregivers, they must learn from attentive listening, and from smelling, touching and manipulating whatever exists within arm's reach. They generally dislike soft toys, and need playthings which provide good 'feelable' shapes and textures and above all a meaningful language. It is comparatively easy for sighted people to shut their own eyes in order to appreciate the grievous deprivations of total blindness; but it is more difficult to understand the baffling visual world of a partially sighted child who may possess some 'patches' of comparatively useful near vision but who has little notion of distances, perspectives or spatial relationships and therefore cannot readily appreciate our predominantly visually organized world.

Blind children are easily distracted by sound. If background noise is too prominent they cannot focus attention on meaningful elements in the environment for long, and so, in self-defence, tend to drift into a state of non-attention, often engaging in the well-known 'blindisms', merely in order to keep themselves in contact with some sort of reality.

Young blind children unable to see how both hands function together may be unaware how to bring this about. Even when bilateral function is explained and illustrated they may still need to feel the position of one hand with the other. If in addition they have a 'central' (cortical) spatial difficulty their learning problems are indescribably complex.

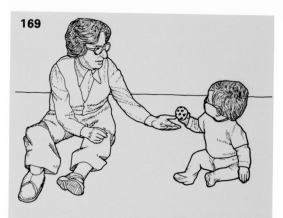

13 months   A partially-sighted baby showing give-and-take play in response to spoken invitation.

22 months   Totally blind boy playing with domestic objects, and correctly naming them.

171 **3½ years** Deaf boy with severe visual handicap playing with miniature toys. Note anticipatory posture of right hand. The miniature toys had no representative value for him. He treated them merely as small manipulative objects.

172 **5 years** A totally blind boy playing on the beach. He is judging the size of his sand castle, by feeling it. His whole posture is very typical.

173 **3¾ years** Partially sighted boy playing with miniature toys. Note that he has grouped all the items of transport in the centre of his array.

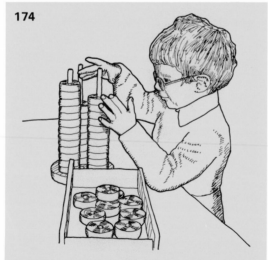

174 **3¾ years** Partially sighted boy playing with an educational toy at eye-level. Note the sensitive hand movements.

175 **5 years** Two musically inclined partially-sighted children, in happy harmony, one singing and the other accompanying her on the xylophone.

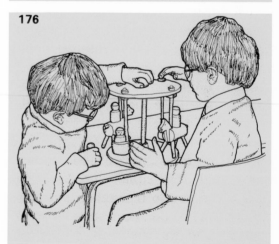

176 **4½ years** Partially sighted children playing with a well-designed educational toy consisting of a mobile roundabout with 'token' horses and pegmen as well as adjustable rods, screws etc.

Children with Seriously Impaired Hearing

Such children must come to terms with people and learn about the world they live in mainly through looking, touching, smelling, exploring and exploiting the environment, and communicating with other people in any way open to them. Although it is essential that they should be properly trained to use whatever residuum of usable hearing they have, and to speak intelligibly, it is only sensible, let alone compassionate, to encourage very young children to employ every available avenue of human communication, including facial expressions, meaningful gestures, pictures, drawings and representative toys ('Wendy-house' size and miniatures) of people, domestic objects, transport, animals etc. Since they do not hear the noises they make it is also sometimes necessary to teach them to appreciate that the rest of us exercise moderation in this regard. It is equally necessary for their caregivers to remember that these children may find the restless, visually overcrowded environment of an ordinary playgroup or nursery school seriously distracting, so that once more, placement requires careful selection, gradual introduction and knowledgeable supervision.

177

2½ years   Intelligent severely deaf boy, playing with the controls of his teacher's portable radio.

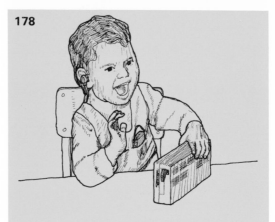

178

At loudness levels intolerable to ordinary listeners he hears a pop-music programme with evident delight.

179

He greatly enjoyed this animal picture inset board, making appropriate noises as he placed the pieces. Here he is saying 'moo'.

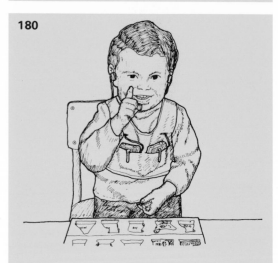

180

The camera flash drew his instant friendly attention to the photographer.

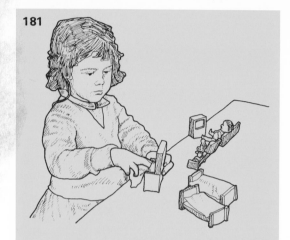

181 **3 years** Severely deaf girl playing with miniature domestic toys. Having seated her dolls in front of the TV, she turned her attention to housework.

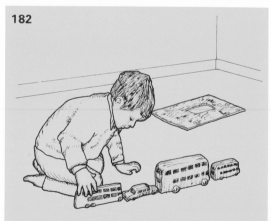

182 **4 years** Deaf boy. Having collected all the available 3-dimensional items of transport, he added a 2-dimensional one from the jig-saw puzzle.

183 **3½ years** Severely deaf girl drawing a completely recognizable face.

184 **7 years** Severely deaf boy drawing a man. Before comprehensive assessment he had been regarded as considerably more mentally retarded than he actually was.

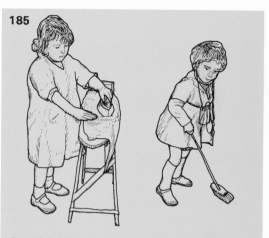

185 **3 and 4 years** Deaf girls in a special nursery unit, engaged in solo-play in contented close proximity.

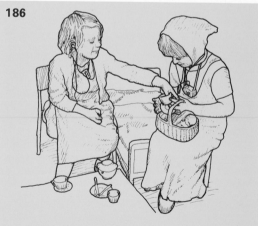

186 The same children playing socially in the Wendy House.

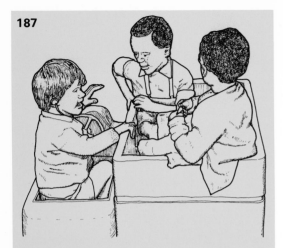

3 and 4 years Three boys all non-speaking (one deaf and the others new immigrants) happily socializing in a day nursery: but nobody is learning to speak.

A charming example of good parental training. The little deaf boy is aged 3 years. In spite of a severe hearing loss he is able to speak several words and phrases.

Children with Other Disorders of Communication

These children present numerous widely-differing and often very serious problems requiring multiprofessional assessment and therapy. The causes of their delayed linguistic development range from lack of normal opportunity to learn, to obscure 'central' brain defects affecting reception, interpretation or expression of language (Sheridan, 1976).

Some children, especially those whose spontaneous use of ordinary playthings provides evidence of good understanding of the everyday world, readily respond to therapeutic intervention. Others, for instance many autistic children, who do not possess any effectual communication code, appear unable to construct mental 'blue-prints' for purposeful movements, although they possess all the necessary neuro-muscular equipment.

Whatever the cause or degree of linguistic disability, it is important to provide opportunities for spontaneous imitative and later inventive play, particularly play which necessitates personal relationships and the use of everyday objects, with strong positive encouragement of simultaneous communication in single words, meaningful vocalizations and 'telling' gestures, however primitive.

Very Deviant Children

Some of the more bizarre manifestation of grossly abnormal motor, sensory, emotional or social development such as apparently purposeless hyperactivity, blindisms, inability to communicate, catastrophic tantrums, autistic withdrawal and the like, can become less bewildering (and hopefully more accessible to therapy) if we regard the afflicted children as helplessly trapped in one of the earlier phases of development. Hence we can argue that some particular handicapped child is still at the mercy of primitive reflexes, or over-reacting to unintegrated perceptual inflow, or showing exploratory insatiability, compulsive clinging to 'transitional objects', inability to establish an effective code of communication, or that his social non-conformity is founded in some deep emotional stress.

In all treatment and training of handicapped children, including 'play therapy', although their *present* attainments must always be considered in relation to normal levels, expectations must never be too securely tied to normal accomplishments. What a child can do (not what he *can't*) *how* he manages to do it, and most importantly of all, whether he can be helped to do it more effectively, are what really matters. Handicapped children referred to special clinics and toy libraries need not only comprehensive assessment but also individual therapeutic prescription regarding playthings. The two requirements are inseparable (Head, 1976; Lear, 1976).

The day-to-day problems of parents of handicapped children have much more in common than in difference, while their advisers need to possess more virtues than compassion and an abundant purse. They must be able to tell the painful truth when parental over-optimism regarding progress is even more unwarranted than over-pessimism. After all, their child is handicapped and for many years will continue to need affection, patient encouragement, and sensible discipline, subject neither to over-protection nor to intolerable strain.

It is my belief that a larger proportion of research into the causes, effects and treatment of children's handicapping conditions, should be conducted in the field rather than in the laboratory. Research workers need to shed many preconceived ideas, to look, listen and record truthfully what is really happening, and not what they theorize from brief observations in structured situations. They must be endowed with intelligence, patience and sensitivity, but above all with that nice combination of insight, foresight and humour that is ordinary common sense.

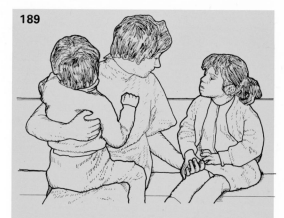

189

Nursery nurse gently encouraging two children aged 3 and 4 years with little or no spoken language, to communicate as best they can in other ways.

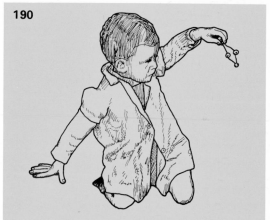

190

4½ years Autistic boy playing with small chime of bells. He sees and hears but lacking any form of language code is unable to communicate with other people.

191

4 years Boy with delayed speech. He sees, hears and understands simple instructions. His very primitive play with common objects and toys indicates mental retardation, later confirmed by psychological tests.

192

4 years Boy with very delayed speech. He sees and hears normally and communicates effectively in gesture. His brisk and sensible play with miniature toys indicates normal intelligence. Provided with timely speech therapy, he rapidly improved.

193

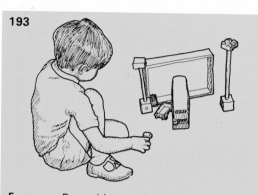

5 years Boy with very delayed speech, who had been living in a multi-lingual environment overseas. He had been in the care of a series of non-English-speaking nannies. He sees and hears normally but communicates only in gestures, jargon and facial expressions. His play was richly inventive.

194

7 years A non-speaking autistic boy with normal vision and hearing but no form of language code. His 'drawing' is merely activity play.

195

7 years Boy with cerebral palsy. He hears, comprehends and uses spoken language but has serious learning problems. He is writing his name under a drawing of a pilot 'in a helicopter'. His visuospatial confusions are clearly obvious.

196

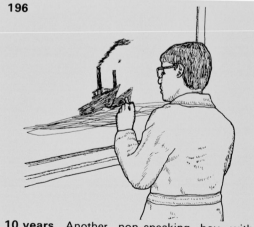

10 years Another non-speaking boy with good comprehension. His seriously defective vision is well-corrected with spectacles. He has notable artistic gifts. His drawing of a ship is in excellent perspective.

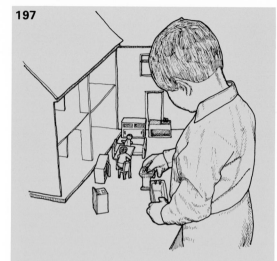

197

3 years Seriously deaf non-speaking boy, demonstrating normal dolls' house play.

198

4¾ years Girl with very limited spoken language, communicating a request for assistance in typical pre-linguistic fashion.

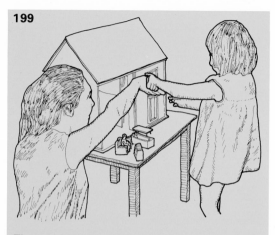

199

The same child moments later. Although physically quite capable of making the necessary movements she does not appear to be capable of programming them ahead.

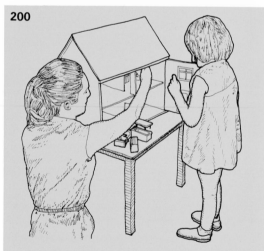

200

She communicates her wish to have all the miniature toys taken out of the house so that she can put them back. She later made good progress with suitable therapy.

201

7 years Boy with very delayed speech and poor comprehension. He is laying out a tidy village street in the manner of a much younger child and repeating softly to himself, 'Houses, houses, houses . . .'

REFERENCES

Connolly, K. and Bruner, J. (1972) *The Growth of Competence*. Academic Press.

Ekecrantz, L. and Rudhe, L. (1972) 'Transitional phenomena', *Acta Scandanavica Psychiatrica*, 48, 261.

Finnie, N. R. (1974) *Handling the Young Cerebral Palsied Child at Home* (2nd edition). London: Heineman.

Freud, S. (1955) *Beyond the Pleasure Principle* (Standard edition). London: Hogarth Press.

Gesell, A. (1954) *The First Five Years of Life*. London: Macmillan.

Head, J. (1976) Personal communication regarding Toy Library Service for handicapped children at Nottingham University Department of Psychology.

Herron, R. E. and Sutton-Smith, B. (editors) (1971) *Child's Play*. Chichester: Wiley.

Lear, Roma (1976) *Play Helps*. Heineman Health Books.

Matterson, E. M. (1965) *Play with a Purpose for the Under-Sevens*. Harmondsworth: Penguin.

Millar, S. (1968) *The Psychology of Play*. Harmondsworth: Penguin.

Morganstern, M., Low-Beer, H. and Morganstern, F. (1966) *Practical Training for the Severely Handicapped*. Spastics Society/Heineman.

Newsom, E. (1974) 'Why toys?' Paper read at meeting of the Royal Society of Medicine, 22nd February 1974.

Owen, R. (editor) (1975) *State of Play*. BBC Publications.

Page, H. (1953) *Playtime in the First Five Years* (2nd edition). London: Allen & Unwin.

Piaget, J. (1951) *Play, Dreams and Imagination in Childhood*. London: Heineman.

Richards, M. P. H. (1974) *Integration of a Child into a Social World*. Cambridge: CUP.

Rosenbloom, L. and Horton, M. E. (1971) 'The maturation of fine prehension', *Developmental Medicine and Child Neurology*, 13, 3–8.

Schaffer, H. R. (editor) (1971) *The Origin of Human Social Relations*. Academic Press.

Sheridan, M. D. (1968) 'Playthings in the development of language', *Health Trends*, 1, 7.

Sheridan, M. D. (1972) 'The child's acquisition of codes for personal and interpersonal communication'. In: Rutter and Martin (editors) *The Child with Delayed Speech*. London: Spastics International.

Sheridan, M. D. (1973) *Children's Developmental Progress: from birth to five years*. Windsor: NFER.

Sonksen, P. M. and Mifsud, A. (1976) 'Development of kick, throw and catch in young children'. Paper at 10th International Study Group on Cerebral Palsy (Spastics Society) at Oxford.

Tizard, B. (1976) *Biology of Play*. SIMP

Most of the books noted provide their own comprehensive reference lists.

Audio-visual Material

Audio-taped lectures (playing time 35–40 minutes) with 48 to 64 colour slides illustrating examinations and behaviour of infants and young children aged from one month to five years (speaker: Mary Sheridan) are available for sale or hire from:

Drs John and Valerie Graves,
MRSF,
Kitts Croft,
Writtle,
Chelmsford, CM1 3EH,
Essex

Several films on child development are available for sale or hire from:

Guild Sound and Vision Ltd.,
Woodston House,
Oundle Road,
Peterborough PE2 9PZ

Devised by Dr Neil O'Doherty:

Neurological Examination of the Full-term Neonate
Child Development: The Six Months Examination
Child Development: The Twelve Months Examination
Child Development: The Two Year Examination

Devised by Dr M. D. Sheridan in collaboration with Professor Neil O'Doherty:

Hearing in the Pre-school Child
Vision in the Pre-school Child
Developmental Aspects of Play
Medical Examination at School Entry

Test Materials Devised by Dr Sheridan and Published by the NFER Publishing Company

The Stycar Chart of Developmental Sequences (Revised Edition 1975)

The Stycar Hearing Tests (Revised Edition 1976)

The Stycar Language Test (1976)

The Stycar Vision Tests (Revised Edition 1968, Panda Test 1973, and Revised Manual 1976)

These tests can only be supplied to appropriately qualified users. Inquiries should be sent to the Test Department, NFER Publishing Company, Darville House, Peascod Street, Windsor, Berks.

Voluntary Agencies: Useful Addresses

Invalid Children's Aid Association (I.C.A.A.),
126 Buckingham Palace Road,
London SW1W 9SB

National Deaf Children's Society,
31 Gloucester Place,
London W1

National Society for Mentally Handicapped Children,
Pembridge Hall,
17 Pembridge Square,
London WC2 4EP

Nursery Schools Association of Gt. Britain and Northern Ireland,
Stamford Street,
London SE1

Pre-School Playgroups Association,
Alford House,
Aveline Street,
London SE11 5DG

Royal National Institute for the Blind (R.N.I.B.),
224–228 Great Portland Street,
London W1N 6AA

Royal National Institute for the Deaf (R.N.I.D.),
105 Gower Street,
London WC1

The Spastics Society,
16 Fitzroy Square,
London W1

Toy Libraries Association,
Sunley House,
Gunthorpe Street,
London E1 7RW